CyberLit

Online Connections to Children's Literature for the Primary Grades

Marilyn Dover Newman

The Scarecrow Press, Inc.
Lanham, Maryland, and Oxford
2004

SCARECROW PRESS, INC.

Published in the United States of America
by Scarecrow Press, Inc.
A wholly owned subsidiary of The Rowman & Littlefield Publishing Group, Inc.
4501 Forbes Boulevard, Suite 200, Lanham, Maryland 20706
www.scarecrowpress.com

PO Box 317
Oxford
OX2 9RU, UK

British Library Cataloguing in Publication Information Available

Library of Congress Cataloging-in-Publication Data

Newman, Marilyn Dover, 1948-
  CyberLit : online connections to children's literature for the primary
grades / Marilyn Dover Newman.
      p. cm.
  Includes bibliographical references and indexes.
  ISBN 0-8108-4903-8 (alk. paper)
  1. Children–Books and reading–United States–Computer network
resources. 2. Children's literature, American–Bio-bibliography–
Computer network resources. 3. Children's literature, American–
Study and teaching (Elementary)–Computer network resources.
4. Illustrated children's books–Computer network resources.
5. Caldecott Medal–Computer network resources. 6. Web sites–
Directories. 7. Internet addresses–Directories. I. Title.
Z1037 .N47 2004
025.06'02855–dc22   2003058744

♾™ The paper used in this publication meets the minimum requirements of
American National Standard for Information Sciences–Permanence of
Paper for Printed Library Materials, ANSI/NISO Z39.48-1992.
Manufactured in the United States of America.

To Stephanie and Michael

Contents

Acknowledgments

This book would not have been possible without the many noteworthy children's literature web sites, author and publisher sites, educators' lesson plans on the World Wide Web, school web sites which include literature units, college and university sites which have posted students' literature-related projects, lesson plan databases, e-bookstores, and search engines, such as *Google*. Although too numerous to list all, there are some sites that deserve special recognition for their outstanding contributions to children's literature:

- Association for Library Service to Children. "Welcome to the Caldecott Medal Home Page," *American Library Association*, http://www.ala.org/Content/NavigationMenu/ALSC/Awards_and_Scholarships1/ Literary_and_Related_Awards/Caldecott_Medal/Caldecott_Medal.htm (30 June 2003).
This site lists the Caldecott Medal and Caldecott Honor Book winners since the inception of the award in 1938.

- Bendall, Linda J. "Linda's Links to Literature," *Richmond Public Schools, Richmond, VA*, http://www.richmond.k12.va.us/readamillion/LITERATURE/lindas_links_to_ literature.htm (30 June 2003).
This is a comprehensive bibliography of books with links to lesson plans and book activities to use in the classroom.

- Bookworm Enterprises. "The Scoop Resource Page," http://www.friend.ly.net/scoop/links/ (30 June 2003).
This site has links to children's literature sites, author sites, online stories, and links to resources for educators and librarians.

- Brown, David K. "The Children's Literature Web Guide," *The University of Calgary*, http://www.acs.ucalgary.ca/~dkbrown/index.html (30 June 2003).
This site features comprehensive links to author and illustrator pages, e-stories on the World Wide Web, *The Douchette Index of Teaching Ideas for Children's Books*, awards, reviews, *Web Travelers' Tool Kit*, resources for teachers, book commentaries, and links to other essential children's literature sites.

- The Children's Book Council. "*CBC*," http://www.cbcbooks.org/index.html (30 June 2003).
This site has archived articles about authors and illustrators, essays about book publishing issues and trends, Author/Editor Dialogues, In the Artist's Studio, and information about book awards and prizes.

- "The de Grummond Children's Literature Collection," *McCain Library and Archives, University of Southern Mississippi*, http://avatar.lib.usm.edu/~degrum/ (30 June 2003).

This site features a scholarly and historical look at children's authors and illustrators with links to rare archived artifacts and original manuscripts.

- Feldman, Roxanne Hsu. "Fairrosa Cyber Library of Children's Literature," http://www.fairrosa.info/ (30 June 2003).
    This site has three major sections: the Reading Room, the Reference Shelf, and the Archives. Each section is subdivided into related topics about children's literature.

- The Horn Book, Inc., "The Horn Book: Publications About Books for Children and Young Adults," http://www.hbook.com/ (30 June 2003).
    This online version of the highly regarded journal takes a scholarly look at children's literature, authors, illustrators, news, issues, trends, and historic aspects. It includes the Boston Globe-Horn Book Awards, both current and past winners.

- Hurst, Carol Otis and Rebecca Otis. "Carol Hurst's Children's Literature Site," http://www.carolhurst.com/index.html (30 June 2003).
    This site features book reviews, curricula connections, activities and lesson plans for children's books, commentary on book themes and authors/illustrators, and reviews with related bibliographies.

- Kerby, Mona. "Mona Kerby's The Reading Corner," *Carroll County Public Library*, http://www.carr.lib.md.us/read/ (30 June 2003).
    This site offers links to author sites, reviews for award books, lists of state award books, and reviews for fiction, nonfiction, picture books, and young adult books.

- Khan, Iram and James Horner. "CanTeach: English Language Arts," *CanTeach.com*, http://www.canteach.ca/links/linkenglish.html (30 June 2003).
    This portion of the site has links to reviews, theme lists, lesson plans, online stories, and authors and illustrators.

- Kiddyhouse. "Literature Based Lesson Plans and Resources," *Kiddyhouse.com*, http://www.kiddyhouse.com/Teachers/ (30 June 2003).
    This site has book-related activities organized by author.

- Lamb, Annette. "Literature Learning Ladders," *Eduscapes.com*, http://eduscapes.com/ladders/ (30 June 2003).
    This site has a wealth of book-related projects, resources for award-winning books, and ideas for technology and literature integration.

- Marilee. "Marilee's Picturebook Links," http://marilee.us/authors.html (30 June 2003).
    This site has links to KidWorks and KidPix book projects, links to authors and illustrators, online picturebooks, recommended book lists, and lesson plans for books.

- Polette, Nancy. "Nancy Polette's Children's Literature Site," *Nancypolette.com*, http://www.nancypolette.com/ (30 June 2003).
  This site offers excellent literature guides for picture books and novel studies, as well as instructional presentation handouts.

- Ramsey, Inez. "The Internet School Library Media Center: Children's Literature and Language Arts Resources," *James Madison University*, http://falcon.jmu.edu/~ramseyil/childlit.htm (30 June 2003).
  This site features links to author and illustrator web sites, biographies, lesson plans, interviews, and reviews, and focuses on children's literature in education.

- Schrock, Kathleen B. "Kathy Schrock's Guide for Educators: Literature and Language Arts," *DiscoverySchool.com*, http://school.discovery.com/schrockguide/arts/artlit.html (30 June 2003).
  This site is among the finest for educators to locate quality web sites relating to children's literature. It offers an array of useful classroom and library media center resources.

- Smith, Cynthia Leitich. "Cynthia Leitich Smith's Children's Literature Resources," http://www.cynthialeitichsmith.com/index1.htm (30 June 2003).
  This site has links to author and illustrator pages, author interviews, bibliographies arranged by reading level and topic, links to guidelines for author visits, and links to e-texts and online stories.

- Vandergrift, Kay E. "Children's Literature Pages," *Rutgers, The State University of New Jersey*, http://scils.rutgers.edu/~kvander/index.html (30 June 2003).
  This prolific, renowned site contains scholarly information about authors, illustrators, children's literature, and book illustration.

These and other sites have been used to gather information for this book. The people who create and maintain these sites are to be commended for their dedication to the subject of children's literature. These sites clearly reveal a devotion to the topic. Their efforts display a desire to communicate the joys of literature to others. Their ideas for using children's literature in classroom situations reflect the premise that literature is alive and well, in fact thriving, in schools across the globe.

There is one other group I would like to acknowledge: the hard-working and dedicated teachers, librarians, and school media specialists who have committed themselves to opening minds to the joys of reading in millions of children everywhere. Their creativity and generosity in sharing ideas is admirable.

When we were very young, some of our fondest memories of elementary school were of our teachers reading aloud to us. We hope that in this fast-paced age of information and technology this memory is not one that will become a thing of the past. Elementary school media specialists and teachers routinely use children's picture books in their lessons. These books add depth and vitality to the curriculum. They are written and illustrated by some of the world's most gifted writers and artists. Their books are truly works of art and are loved by millions of adults and children all over the world. Their works will be with us long after our students leave us. And yet, educators are finding it increasingly harder to insert this pleasant and important activity into the busy school day due to increased pressures to improve test scores, implement a standards-driven curriculum, and stay abreast of new technologies to deliver instruction. This book seeks to help educators continue to incorporate literature into the school day in spite of the obstacles they face and the pressures of accountability.

This work is a compilation of outstanding children's author websites, children's literature websites, and notable storybook character websites that go beyond the ordinary. The information has already been searched, collected, assessed, and compiled. There is no more need to get lost in cyberspace. At one's fingertips, this directory can help teachers get biographical information about authors and illustrators, learn how authors get ideas for stories, how books are made, how illustrations are created, how to extend the books within the framework of the curriculum, and where to go to find time-saving, recommended lesson plans and book-related activities for classroom projects and units. This book is for those who work with, or teach others who work with, children in the primary grades. It is for those who use trade books to supplement and enhance health, science, creative writing, history, geography, reading, math, language arts, character education, multicultural studies, holidays, citizenship, and the fine arts. It is for those who love children's literature and book illustration.

Many children's authors have begun to originate their own websites—some are quite impressive. Some authors have sites associated with their publishing companies, which are not as new but still offer curricular connections for teachers. Many of the sites hold nice surprises for busy educators. They are little gems in cyberspace waiting to be discovered, explored, and shared. They offer many uses for the classroom. However, dozens of well-known author sites have been examined only to find that many were simply marketing devices to sell books. Even some personal favorites did not meet the criteria used to select sites for inclusion in this book.

The sites chosen have educational value and a minimum of commercialization. They go beyond the ordinary. They are exemplary examples of authors, publishers, or scholars who understand and acknowledge the roles of teachers and librarians: that they teach through literature, they strive to engage and motivate children to read, and they seek ways to combine literature studies with the content areas. Authors and publishers realize that educators use their works not only from which to read aloud, but also for meaningful extension activities for skill building, improving reading comprehension and supplementing, even supplanting, textbooks. The sites were chosen because they include pages especially for teachers and librarians. They provide a wealth of ancillary information to enhance literature units and author studies. They were also chosen because the authors did not forget that children are also users of their sites. They have included features to help students learn more about the world of books. Perusal of the sites can lead to a heightened awareness and appreciation of literature, the power of language, and the beauty of art. These websites can be valuable tools to be used to help teach and augment many of the same things we have traditionally taught, but in a new, more exciting way.

Will today's children look back upon their school years and remember their teachers reading aloud to the class? Yes, as long as educators acknowledge the power of those books in the educational process, and, as long as authors continue to produce quality works that validate the use of their works by educators. Will students' aesthetic appreciation of literature be enriched from these experiences? Yes, but perhaps subconsciously at first. When students reach adulthood, it will become more apparent to them if they continue to pursue reading as a pastime. Adults who love to read were probably read to when they were young. Adults will normally widen the scope of their reading tastes to include works considered to be higher levels of literary achievement. This is more likely to happen if their teachers planted those seeds of interest in books and appreciation of literature.

If educators are using technology for the delivery of instruction in the content areas, might they also enhance literature studies through technology? Yes, they can. Can authors and publishers also use technology as a tool to approach educators and to reach out to children? Absolutely they can. Those who are doing so should be commended for adding a new dimension to literary explorations. Using the power of the World Wide Web is bringing virtual author visits to schools and opening up new possibilities for exchanging information globally. Classroom walls are no longer a barrier to the information that awaits our students.

A "five-apple" rating scale for the sites was devised to portray the comprehensiveness of information, educational value and usefulness to educators, appeal to students, age appropriateness, visual attractiveness, audio and video enhancements, evidence of curricular connections, technologically friendly, active and correct hyperlinks, ease of navigation, frequency of updating, and inclusion of interactive features, downloads, and printables for classroom use. The degree of generosity of the authors and publishers in sharing their resources with educators was also taken into account. The rating scale ranges from three to five apples: five apples = outstanding, four = superior, and three = above average. No sites were included which were deemed average and below average.

The chapters in the book have been organized in this manner:
- Description of the web site
- Best of site: most valuable feature for educators
- Special features of the web site for educators and students
- About the author: biographical information
- Online author studies: where to go to get more information about the author
- Internet links to lesson plans to use with specific titles
- Classroom center ideas for online or offline activities

The Jan Brett Website

Welcome to Jan Brett's Home Page

http://www.janbrett.com

Description of Site

Your cursor turns into a magic wand, complete with glittering stars, as you move through this remarkable site. Surprises unfold with each click of the mouse, carrying you on an educator's dream journey through the beautiful pages. Jan Brett has elevated cyberspace to a commendable level. The site offers an astounding array of resources and ideas to support and enhance an integrated curriculum. Ms. Brett's trademark illustrations are prolific throughout the site and lend themselves to an array of uses for the classroom. The site contains over 1200 pages of artwork and activities. A bibliography with links to annotations and reviews is available, as well as links to lesson ideas and cross-curricular activities. Jan Brett is to be complimented for her outstanding site and her generosity to share printable activities for classroom use. The site is frequently updated and new surprises await us each time we visit.

Best of Site: Piggybacks for Teachers and Librarians

This section offers curriculum-based projects and activities to correlate with Jan Brett's books and their themes. Each featured title has suggestions for using the books in an integrated curriculum. There are extensions for math, science, social studies, language arts, and art. Many of the activities have printable worksheets, puzzles, coloring sheets, or games to enhance teaching through literature.

Lesson plan ideas in this chapter...	Special features of site...
◆ *Berlioz the Bear*	◆ Monthly Hedge-a-Gram
◆ *The Gingerbread Baby*	◆ Interactive Games and Coloring
◆ *The Hat*	◆ Video and Audio Clips
◆ *The Mitten*	◆ E-cards and Stationery

About the Author

Jan Brett is the renowned illustrator and writer of children's picture books and re-teller of popular folktales and fairy tales. Classically trained in fine art at the Boston Museum School, Ms. Brett's works are impressively filled with detail to setting, characters, costumes, and objects. She provides nuances about a country in her illustrations, such as details in landscape and architecture. She creates beautiful borders and side panels in her books that reveal an added dimension to her stories. Before embarking on a new book, Ms. Brett spends hours researching and traveling to give authenticity to her illustrations and to ensure that her settings are historically accurate. Ms. Brett's lovely works of art, for that is what they are, are surely destined to become classics in children's literature.

Online Author Studies

- Brett, Jan. "About Jan Brett," *Welcome to Jan Brett's Home Page*,
  http://www.janbrett.com/biography.htm (29 June 2003).
  This biographical sketch, with photograph, contains links to audio and video clips of the author as she talks about her works.

- Costales, Mary. "Piggybacks for Teachers: Internet Author Study," *Welcome to Jan Brett's Home Page*,
  http://janbrett.com/piggybacks/piggybacks_internet_author_study.htm
  (29 June 2003).
  This author study offers information about the author and her works.

- "Meet Jan Brett," *Scholastic, Inc.*,
  http://www2.scholastic.com/teachers/authorsandbooks/authorstudies/author
  home.jhtml?authorID=13&collateralID=5110&displayName=Biography
  (29 June 2003).
  This site has an interview conducted by students and a bibliography of works.

- Morris, Loretta, Patty Dillon, and Mary Ann Boyles. "I Lost My Mitten, It's in My Hat," *Ronceverte Elementary, Greenbrier County*,
  http://www.thesolutionsite.com/lpnew/lesson/1411/ronceverte2elA.html
  (29 June 2003).
  This six-part unit has an author study and individual lessons for *Berlioz the Bear*, *The Mitten*, *The Hat*, *The Trouble with Trolls*, and *The Gingerbread Baby*. Each lesson has links to help students find information.

Lesson Plan Ideas

Berlioz the Bear

> Annotation: Berlioz and his fellow orchestra members are on their way to perform at a Bavarian village ball when a wagon wheel gets stuck in a pothole in the road. Children will delight over the antics of the animals as they try to get the uncooperative donkey to pull the wagon out of the hole. [Putnam, 1991, hardcover ISBN: 0399222480]

- Brett, Jan. "Newsnotes: Berlioz the Bear," *Welcome to Jan Brett's Home Page*,
  http://www.janbrett.com/newsnotes/berlioz_newsnotes2.htm (29 June 2003).
  Read Ms. Brett's illustrated notes about how she got her ideas for this story.

- Dallas Symphony Orchestra Association. "Families of the Orchestra,"
  http://www.dsokids.com/2001/instrumentchart.htm (30 June 2003).
  This well-done site can be used to extend the book to learn more about musical instruments. Each instrument is linked to an article. Be sure to click on the "Kids" section for online games and activities about music. Students can look up the instruments that were illustrated in the story.

- Lux, Kevin. "Learn about the Instruments," *Data Dragon Information Services*,
  http://datadragon.com/education/instruments/ (30 June 2003).
  This site lets students listen to the sounds of different instruments. This would be a good activity to use with the book.

- "Piggybacks for Teachers: Berlioz the Bear," *Welcome to Jan Brett's Home Page*,
  http://www.janbrett.com/piggybacks/piggybacks_berlioz_the_bear.htm
  (29 June 2003).
  This page has good ideas for cross-curricular activities to extend the book.

- Wilborne, Shirley. "Reading Comprehension Quiz: Berlioz the Bear," *Park Avenue Elementary School, Danbury Public Schools, VA*,
  http://web.dps.k12.va.us/ParkAve/berlioz.htm (29 June 2003).
  This printable quiz can be used to check students' comprehension and vocabulary. It can also be used online as an interactive quiz with hints and feedback.

The Gingerbread Baby

> Annotation: Matti opens the oven to check on the gingerbread a little too soon. Out pops a gingerbread baby. His antics delight the reader as he roams through the Swiss village. Does the same fate await him as in the traditional story, *The Gingerbread Boy*? The illustrations are vintage Brett, complete with intricate borders and a Swiss theme throughout. [Putnam, 1999, hardcover ISBN: 0399234446]

- Brett, Jan. "Newsnotes: The Gingerbread Baby," *Welcome to Jan Brett's Home Page*,
  http://www.janbrett.com/newsnotes/gingerbread_baby_newsnotes_page_1.htm
  (29 June 2003).
  Read the author's illustrated notes about how she got her ideas for this version.

- DeBoer, Kelley. "Gingerbread Baby Literature Unit," *A to Z Teacher Stuff*,
  http://www.atozteacherstuff.com/lessons/GingerbreadBabyList.shtml
  (29 June 2003).
  This impressive unit has eleven lessons to use with the story. Each lesson is linked to a separate lesson plan. Activities include learning about literary elements, strengthening vocabulary, comparing and contrasting, practicing map skills, and creating art activities. The culminating activity is a Jan Brett party.

The Hat

> Annotation: This heartwarming story begins as Hedgie the hedgehog sniffs a woolen stocking that has fallen off the clothesline. The other farm animals gather around Hedgie and laugh at him as he gets stuck in the stocking because of his prickles. The setting is the Scandinavian countryside in winter. The book is the 1998 winner of the Boston Globe-Horn Book Award. [Putnam, 1997, hardcover ISBN: 0399231013]

- Brett, Jan. "Newsnotes: The Hat," *Welcome to Jan Brett's Home Page*,
  http://www.janbrett.com/newsnotes/the_hat_newsnotes_page_1.htm
  (29 June 2003).
  Read Ms. Brett's background information and inspiration for writing this book.

- Bruner, Judy. "The Hedgehog Travel Buddy Project: Activities for *The Hat*," *Elementary West, Loogootee, IN*, http://www.siec.k12.in.us/~west/proj/hedge/hatbook.htm (29 June 2003).
This site offers activities for each day of the week. Many of the activities have links to help students complete them.

- "Frosty Readers' Project: The Hat," *Miss Brown's Second Grade Class, T. Baldwin Demarest School, Old Tappan, NJ*, http://www.kids-learn.org/frosty/baldwin.htm (29 June 2003).
This site has creative writing activities illustrated with pictures of students' artwork. There is a link to a readers' theatre script for the story.

- "Frosty Readers' Project: The Hat," *Mrs. Harrison's Second Grade Class, St. Thomas Aquinas, Calgary, Alberta*, http://www.kids-learn.org/frosty/thomas.htm (29 June 2003).
This site shows examples of students' poetry and writing created to extend the story.

- Marie, Theresa. "Piggybacks for Teachers: The Hat," *Welcome to Jan Brett's Home Page*, http://www.janbrett.com/piggybacks/hat.htm
There are many links to cross-curricular activities to extend this book, learn more about hedgehogs, and learn about Denmark, the setting for the book.

The Mitten

> Annotation: Nicki asks his grandmother to knit him a pair of white mittens even though it is against her better judgment in case they get lost in the snow. Of course, Nicki does lose one of his mittens. One-by-one, the forest animals discover the mitten and try to snuggle into it for warmth. This humorous Ukrainian tale will keep students laughing as they see the mitten stretch. [Putnam, 1989, hardcover ISBN: 039921920X]

- Adams, Jane and Kim Howard. "The Mitten," *Teachers.net*, http://www.teachers.net/lessons/posts/456.html (29 June 2003).
This lesson effectively integrates technology with literature. After reading the book, students will use the character masks from the author's web site for dramatic play, write an online letter to the author, and complete a web site evaluation.

- Brett, Jan. "Newsnotes: The Mitten," *Welcome to Jan Brett's Home Page*, http://www.janbrett.com/newsnotes/mitten_newsnotes2.htm (29 June 2003).
Read Ms. Brett's background information and inspiration for writing this book.

- "Frosty Readers' Project: The Mitten," *Mr. Francis' Class, Attica Elementary School, Attica, MI,* http://www.kids-learn.org/frosty/attica.htm (29 June 2003).
  This site displays students' illustrated short stories from the animals' points of view.

- "Frosty Readers' Project: The Mitten," *Mrs. Powell and Mrs. Rice's Second Grade Classes, Endy Elementary School, Albemarle, NC,* http://www.kids-learn.org/frosty/endy.htm (29 June 2003).
  This site displays students' acrostic poetry and a delightful animated "Designer Mitten Show." Use this idea to have students design their own designer mittens.

- Haynes, Judie. "Who's Inside the Mitten?" *EverythingESL.net,* http://www.everythingesl.net/lessons/janbrett_mitten.php (29 June 2003).
  This lesson plan links to the game "Put the Animals in the Mitten" and animal masks. There is a play script, which can be used to practice sequencing.

- Hurst, Carol and Rebecca Otis. "The Mitten," *Carol Hurst's Children's Literature Site,* http://www.carolhurst.com/titles/mitten.html (29 June 2003).
  This site has good suggestions for extending the book in the classroom through discussions of the illustration details, a thesaurus study of verbs, and links to other sites about Jan Brett and the themes from the book.

- "Jan Brett Winter Books: The Mitten," *TeacherVision.com, The Learning Network,* http://www.teachervision.com/lesson-plans/lesson-4092.html (29 June 2003).
  This unit has an excellent art activity to help students understand the role of borders in Jan Brett's books.

- Lloyd, Jennifer. "Be a Forest Animal Web Site Detective," *Welcome to Jan Brett's Home Page,* http://www.janbrett.com/piggybacks/forest_animal_website_detective.htm (29 June 2003).
  Students will enjoy this webquest to learn more about the forest animals from the story. They will access other web sites about forest animals, then complete the table.

- Mehl, Sheron. "Teacher CyberGuide: The Mitten," *San Diego County Office of Education,* http://www.sdcoe.k12.ca.us/score/mit/mittg.html (29 June 2003).
  This online project utilizes the Jan Brett web site to learn how the author got her ideas for the book, write in journals and create borders, do an e-mail activity, and use the character masks for dramatization of the story.

Jan Brett Library Media Center Activity

Name _____

Directions: Find where Jan Brett's books are located in your library. Use the online catalog to look up each of these titles, then write the call number for each book. When finished, go to the bookshelves to see if the book is on the shelf. Place a ✓ (check mark) in the blanks.

1. *Armadillo Rodeo*   Call Number _____
   ___My library has this book.
   ___My library does not have this book.
   ___I found the book on the shelf.
   ___I did not find the book on the shelf.

2. *Berlioz the Bear*   Call Number _____
   ___My library has this book.
   ___My library does not have this book.
   ___I found the book on the shelf.
   ___I did not find the book on the shelf.

3. *The Gingerbread Baby*   Call Number _____
   ___My library has this book.
   ___My library does not have this book.
   ___I found the book on the shelf.
   ___I did not find the book on the shelf.

4. *The Hat*   Call Number _____
   ___My library has this book.
   ___My library does not have this book.
   ___I found the book on the shelf.
   ___I did not find the book on the shelf.

5. *The Mitten*   Call Number _____
   ___My library has this book.
   ___My library does not have this book.
   ___I found the book on the shelf.
   ___I did not find the book on the shelf.

Jan Brett Teaching Aids for Teachers

- Birthday Calendars
  http://www.janbrett.com/birthday_calendar/birthday_calendar_main.htm

- Bookmarks
  http://www.janbrett.com/bookmarks/bookmarks.htm
  Select from bookmarks for Jan Brett's books or holidays.

- Bookplate
  http://www.janbrett.com/bookplate.htm

- Bulletin Board Accessories
  http://www.janbrett.com/activities_pages.htm
  (See "B" for bulletin board on the site map.) Select from borders, Dolch word lists, manuscript or cursive alphabets, days, months, numbers, etc.

- Calendars
  http://www.janbrett.com/calendars.htm
  Download, print, and bind the monthly artwork and monthly grids to make a classroom calendar, or complete the grids online, then print.

- Cards and Stationery
  http://www.janbrett.com/activities_pages.htm
  (Go to "C" for Cards and "S" for Stationery.)

- Certificates
  http://www.janbrett.com/awards/awards_main.htm
  Honor students with a variety of achievement awards.

- Cross Stitch Patterns
  http://www.janbrett.com/cross_stitch/cross_stitch_patterns_main_page.htm

- Flashcards
  http://www.janbrett.com/activities_pages.htm
  (See "F" for flashcards.) Select from addition, subtraction, multiplication, division, colors, numbers, shapes, sight words, etc.

More Teaching Aids for Teachers

- Games
  http://www.janbrett.com/games/games_main.htm

- Iron-on Transfers
  http://www.janbrett.com/iron_on_transfers.htm

- Lesson Planner
  http://www.janbrett.com/planner/planner1.php4
  Print blank pages or plan online, then print.

- Name Plates
  http://www.janbrett.com/hedgie_name_plate.htm

- Name Tags
  http://www.janbrett.com/hedgie_name_tags.htm

- Placemats
  http://www.janbrett.com/place_mats/party_place_mats_main.htm
  Select from party, spring, and Christmas placemats.

- Puzzles: Addition and Subtraction
  http://www.janbrett.com/games/janbretts_addition_and_subtraction_main.htm

- Recipes
  http://www.janbrett.com/cgi/recipes.pl
  Select from 1800 recipes by category.

- Screensavers
  http://www.janbrett.com/screensaver.htm

- Secret Santa Selections
  http://www.janbrett.com/secret_santa_selections.htm

- Stickers
  http://www.janbrett.com/hedgie_stickers.htm

Fun with Jan Brett's Web Site

Materials: computer with Internet access, printer, crayons or colored pencils, display of Jan Brett's books.

- Coloring Pages
  http://www.janbrett.com/activities_pages_artwork.htm

- Jan Brett Interactive Coloring Pages
  http://www.janbrett.com/coloring_applet/jan_brett_coloring.htm
  (Internet Explorer required.)

- Send an E-Postcard
  http://www.janbrett.com/vcards/

- Play Hedgie's Scrambler Game
  http://www.janbrett.com/games/hedgie_and_henny_puzzle.htm

- Hedgie's Book-a-Matic
  http://www.janbrett.com/bookamatic/hedgies_book_a_matic.htm
  Take an online survey to find the perfect Jan Brett book for you.

- Design Your Own Jan Brett Gingerbread Baby House
  http://www.janbrett.com/trim_a_jan_brett_gingerbread_baby_house.htm

- Design Your Own Jan Brett Christmas Tree
  http://www.janbrett.com/trim_a_jan_brett_christmas_tree.htm

- Write a Letter with Interactive Stationery
  http://www.janbrett.com/jan_brett_interactive_stationery.htm
  Print your letter when you are finished.

- Play Mouse Concentration Game
  http://www.janbrett.com/piggybacks/mouse_concentration.htm

- View Jan Brett's Video Clips
  http://www.janbrett.com/video/video_main_page.htm

- Complete *The Hat* Online Graphing Activity
  http://www.janbrett.com/hat_graph.htm

© Permissions

Caution should be used when downloading, printing, displaying, and using the artwork and text from the Jan Brett website. Consult the author's Terms of Use Agreement: "Jan Brett grants to you a non-exclusive license to use and display for your personal use the artwork and text on these pages, and to download and print materials available through these pages, all solely for your personal, classroom, or library non-commercial use. You may create as many copies as you wish, but you may not transfer, assign, sub-license, or sell the rights granted under this license. This license permits the display and printing of the artwork and text on your personal, school, or library computer, but not the re-use or incorporation or framing of the artwork or text on another Internet site or email list or for use in any promotion or advertisement or on any product for which a charge is made."

✉ Making Contact

Teachers and librarians can write for a Teacher Pack:
Jan Brett
P. O. Box 336
Nowell, MA 02061

E-mail:
http://www.janbrett.com/email.html

Sign up for *Hedgie's Online Newsletter*:
http://www.janbrett.com/list/subscribe.htm

Sign up for Jan Brett's Reminder Service:
(Select dates and times to receive an e-mail reminder with Jan Brett artwork.)
http://www.janbrett.com/r103/signup.php

Marc Brown's Arthur

Arthur and Friends

http://pbskids.org/arthur/

Description of Site

Marc Brown and WGBH Educational Foundation have created a powerful web site. Within this site are multiple pages for all of Marc Brown's beloved characters. Each character's "homepage" is filled with activities, music, contests, coloring pages, poetry, and games guaranteed to generate ideas for use in the classroom or library media center. There are also pages devoted to "Grownups." Links are abundant for information about the author, lists of Marc Brown's books, and descriptions of the companion television programs with teachers' guides for curriculum integration activities. This web site is sure to be a hit with educators who are seeking ways to motivate their students to read.

Best of Site: The Letter Writer Helper

Located on "Arthur's Postcards Page," this section offers a wealth of instructional information for students on letter writing. It includes topics about what makes a good letter, what goes on an envelope, suggestions for dealing with junk mail, how e-mail works, how regular mail works, and a list of emoticons. In addition, students can read interesting facts about the history of paper, stamps, and the Pony Express. This section of the web site is would be helpful for the language arts curriculum.

Lesson plan ideas in this chapter...	Special features of site...
◆ *Arthur Meets the President*	◆ D. W.'s Online Art Studio
◆ *Arthur's New Puppy*	◆ Francine's Play-Maker
◆ *Arthur's Eyes*	◆ Interactive Games
◆ *D. W. the Picky Eater*	◆ Character Masks

About the Author

Marc Brown, author and illustrator of the popular *Arthur* series, has contributed greatly to children's enjoyment of books and reading. He began drawing as a boy and later studied art at the Cleveland Art Institute. He published his first book, *Arthur's Nose*, in 1976 and since has written dozens of books for children. Many of his books have been made into videos. The inspiration for many of Mr. Brown's stories come from his own childhood and the experiences he had with his family and friends. He writes with insight about the everyday fears and problems that children encounter as they grow up. He collaborates with PBS to develop the equally popular *Arthur* television series. His influence continues with a new generation.

Online Author Studies

- "About Marc Brown," *Arthur and Friends, PBSKids.org*,
    http://pbskids.org/arthur/grownups/ (28 June 2003).
  Click on "About Marc Brown" to access a biography and answers to questions.

- "Author Bios: Marc Brown," *Teachers' Resource Center, Random House Online, Inc.*, http://www.randomhouse.com/teachers/rc/rc_ab_mbr.html
    (28 June 2003).
  This site has biographical information about Marc Brown and a link to the Random House *Arthur* pages with online activities and printables.

- "EPA's Top 100 Authors: Marc Brown," *Educational Paperback Association*,
    http://www.edupaperback.org/showauth.cfm?authid=16 (28 June 2003).
  This site has a detailed autobiographical statement from the author.

- "Get to Know Marc Brown," *The Scoop, Bookworm Enterprises*,
    http://www.friend.ly.net/scoop/biographies/brownmarc/ (28 June 2003).
  This site has colorful photographs of the author and details about his life and works.

- Harms, Janet. "Marc Brown, Author and Illustrator," *Louisiana Challenge Activities for the K-12 Classroom*,
    http://www.challenge.state.la.us/edres/lessons/elementary/lesson3.htm
    (28 June 2003).
  This author study helps students learn more about Marc Brown through explorations with his books and web site. There is a K-W-L activity sheet included.

- Monastersky, Tera. "Arthur," *Michigan State University*,
    http://www.msu.edu/~monaster/ArthurLessonPlanUnitIndex.htm (28 June 2003).

This six-part lesson plan helps students learn about the author, get to know the popular aardvark character, write and illustrate a story, critique the stories, and explore Arthur's Internet sites.

- "Scholastic Authors Online: Meet Marc Brown," *Scholastic, Inc.*,
     http://www2.scholastic.com/teachers/authorsandbooks/authorstudies/authorhome
     .jhtml?authorID=15&collateralID=5112&displayName=Biography
     (28 June 2003).
Read a biography and an in-depth interview with Marc Brown.

Lesson Plan Ideas

Arthur Meets the President

> Annotation: Arthur's essay, "How to Help Make America Great," wins a contest and the prize is a trip to Washington, D.C., to meet the President. Arthur will recite his essay on television to millions of viewers. He learns a valuable lesson about how to really help make America great. [Little, Brown Children's Books, 1991, hardcover ISBN: 0316112658]

- Harvey, Linda. "TeacherView: Arthur Meets the President," *Education Place, Houghton Mifflin Company*,
     http://www.eduplace.com/tview/tviews/a/arthurmeetsthepresident.html
     (27 June 2003).
This lesson plan has students write an essay similar to the one Arthur wrote, but with the topic "How to Help Make our School Great." There is also an introduction to Washington, D.C. for students.

- WGBH Web Activities. "Welcome to Washington, D.C.," *Arthur and Friends, PBS.org*,
     http://pbskids.org/arthur/grownups/activities/web/welcome_washington.html
     (27 June 2003).
Use the book and the television episode, "D. W. Goes to Washington," as the basis for this lesson plan. Students will learn about Washington, D.C., and create travel brochures. There is a link to the official White House site.

- "The White House for Kids," *Whitehousekids.gov*, http://www.whitehouse.gov/kids/
     (28 June 2003).
This is a must-see site to explore the Office of the Presidency and the White House.

Arthur's New Puppy

Annotation: Arthur gets a new puppy and promises his skeptical parents he will take care of it. Can the household survive this frisky new member of the family? [Bargain, 1993, hardcover ISBN: 0316113557]

- "Arthur's New Puppy Word Search," *Ameritech.net*,
    http://www.ameritech.net/users/macler2/2wsMBpuppy.gif (27 June 2003).
Enlarge and print this word puzzle to use after reading the story. Students must fill in the blanks prior to completing the puzzle.

- "Best Friends Schoolhouse," *Best Friends Animal Sanctuary*,
    http://bestfriends.org/nmhp/school/clresources.htm (28 June 2003).
This is an excellent site to get information on pets, pet care, lesson plans for teachers, and much more. Use this site in conjunction with the book.

- "Care for Animals," *The American Veterinary Medical Association*,
    http://www.avma.org/careforanimals/default.asp (28 June 2003).
This site has pet care information, an animated tutorial, and a Kids' Corner with games, puzzles, and activity sheets about pets.

- Ellison, Becky. "Arthur's New Puppy: Directed Reading Lesson," *Teachers.net*
    Lesson Bank, http://www.teachers.net/lessons/posts/475.html
    (27 June 2003).
This lesson has a pre-reading activity to help students brainstorm what Arthur needs to do before he gets his new puppy. Students also visit the *Arthur and Friends* web site and will compose a class letter to Arthur.

- Shockey, Dinah. "Discovering Marc Brown," *Montgomery County Public Schools*,
    http://www.mcps.k12.md.us/departments/isa/elit/el/arthurless.htm
    (27 June 2003).
This unit helps students learn more about the author and his characters. Students use a Venn diagram to compare two stories by Marc Brown, *Arthur's New Puppy* and *Arthur's Nose*. There is a link to a Venn diagram.

Arthur's Eyes

> Annotation: Arthur hates having to wear glasses. His friends tease him so he tries to do without them. But he soon learns a valuable lesson about having to wear glasses. [Little, Brown Children's Books, 1979, hardcover ISBN: 0316110639]

- "Arthur's Eyes," *Nashville Public Schools, TN*,
  http://www.nashville.k12.tn.us/CurriculumAwards/PercyPriest/Questions_
  Arthur's_Eyes.html (28 June 2003).
  This site has discussion questions to use with the book.

- Coffey, Jaime. "Arthur's Eyes," *Powerof2.org*,
  http://www.powerof2.org/resources/elementary/reading/arthur/ (28 June 2003).
  This site has worksheets and a quiz to use with the story.

- Reading Rainbow. "Teachers Activities: Arthur's Eyes," *GPN*,
  http://gpn.unl.edu/guides/rr/13.pdf (27 June 2003).
  This guide has many activities which discuss vision health, glasses, the sense of sight, Braille, and a graphing activity for students' eye colors.

- "Marina's Guide to Braille and More," *Arthur and Friends*, *PBSkids.org*,
  http://pbskids.org/arthur/print/braille/braille_guide.html (27 June 2003).
  This page from the *Arthur* web site explains Braille to children and how it helps people who are blind. Click on "Braille Translator" for a fun activity to see words transformed into Braille. To extend this lesson further, go to these sections of the *Arthur and Friends* site:
  - "Communication Exploration: Blindness" at:
    http://pbskids.org/arthur/grownups/teacherguides/communication/blindness.html
  - See the activity, "Eye to Eye," which can be accessed at:
    http://pbskids.org/arthur/grownups/activities/play_learn1/eye_eye.html
  - View episode #101, "Arthur's Eyes"
  - View episode #709, "Prunella Sees the Light"

- Vilendrer, Barb. "Who Is Marc Brown?" *Manteno County Public Schools, IL*,
  http://www.manteno.k12.il.us/ (27 June 2003).
  To access this webquest, click on "WebQuests" from the main menu, then "Elementary WebQuests." This activity will help students learn more about Marc Brown while reading *Arthur's Eyes*. Students will enjoy making Arthur's glasses. A pattern is included.

D. W. the Picky Eater

> Annotation: D. W., Arthur's little sister, is a very fussy eater. Dining out is an unpleasant experience for her whole family until she is invited to a fancy restaurant for her grandmother's birthday. She orders the Little Bo Peep Pot Pie and discovers that it is actually quite delicious. [Little, Brown Children's Books, 1995, hardcover ISBN: 0316109576]

- "Let's Read! D. W. the Picky Eater," *Texas Department of Health*, http://www.tdh.state.tx.us/kids/lessonplans/dw_eng.htm (28 June 2003).

  This detailed lesson plan provides information to teachers and parents suggesting ways to deal with a picky eater. The site has handouts and questions to use with the story. Use the story as an introduction to a unit on nutrition.

- WBGH Web Activities. "Potluck Pyramid," *Arthur and Friends, PBS.org*, http://pbskids.org/arthur/grownups/activities/web/potluck_pyramid.html (28 June 2003).

  This activity lets students create a food pyramid to learn more about nutrition and the five food groups. Use after reading the book or viewing television episode #203, "D. W. the Picky Eater."

© Permissions

Read the copyright link at the bottom of the *Arthur and Friends* homepage to see the permissions and restrictions for using this site. One copy of each download is permitted per computer station for personal and non-commercial use and printouts must be accompanied by the copyright notices.

⊠ Making Contact

Write to:
Marc Brown
c/o Little, Brown, and Company
3 Center Plaza
Boston, MA 02108

E-mail: arthur@wgbh.org

To request print materials:
Arthur Guides
Educational Print and Outreach
WGBH
125 Western Avenue
Boston, MA 02134

Fern's Poetry Club Activity

Name _____

Directions: Go to "Fern's Poetry Club":
http://pbskids.org/arthur/games/poetry/

1. Click on "What's a Poem?" and list the six kinds of poems and a brief definition to explain each kind:

_____   _____

_____   _____

_____   _____

_____   _____

_____   _____

_____   _____

2. Click on the link for each kind of poem and read the example.

3. Which one of the six kinds of poems did you like best and why?

   My favorite kind of poem is _____

   because_____.

4. Read poems from other children by clicking on "Read More Poems."

   Vote for your favorite poem: _____

5. Write your own poem. Practice first on a blank sheet of paper. Then go to "Write a Poem" on the web site and fill in the blanks. Print your poem when you are finished and turn it in to your teacher.

For Librarians and School Library Media Specialists

- Bookmarks: **http://pbskids.org/arthur/print/bookmarks/index.html**

- "Arthur's 100 Book Celebration": view reading motivation activities
  http://pbskids.org/arthur/grownups/events/hundred_books.html

- "Favorite Books": see the characters' recommended book lists
  http://pbskids.org/arthur/grownups/favoritebooks/index.html

- "Francine's Play-maker": put on the play, "D. W. Gets her Library Card"
  http://pbskids.org/arthur/print/playmaker/script/

- The following are language and literacy activities from the *Arthur* web site:
  http://pbskids.org/arthur/grownups/activities/language.html
  - "A is for Arthur!": learn about alphabetical order and letters of the alphabet
  - "Arthur's Reading Tips": improve independent reading skills
  - "Author! Author!": tips on writing and illustrating a story
  - "Be a Book Critic": learn about reviewing books
  - "Black and White and Read All Over": learn about newspapers
  - "Book Brunch": pledge to read more and watch less tv
  - "Discussing Arthur Books and Videos": help with settings and characters
  - "Check it Out": learn about the library
  - "Hold a Film Festival": make pretend movies for books
  - "Lights, Camera, Action!": learn about folktales and make a play
  - "Poet's Corner": appreciating poetry
  - "Publishing Stories": storytelling activities for the classroom
  - "Secret Character Game": learn about characterization in stories
  - "The Story Map": learn about the elements in a story

- "Welcome to the Web": exploring the Internet safely and responsibly
  http://pbskids.org/arthur/grownups/parentguides/web.index.html

- The following *Arthur* episodes have book or library-related themes:
  - #104 "Arthur's Lost Library Book"
  - #106 "Locked in the Library"
  - #128 "I'm a Poet"
  - #207 "Arthur's TV-Free Week"
  - #211 "Buster Hits the Books"
  - #302 "I'd Rather Read it Myself"
  - #401 "D. W.'s Library Card"
  - #406 "D. W. Tale Spins"
  - #601 "Best of the Nest"
  - #603 "Prunella's Special Edition"

Classroom Center Ideas

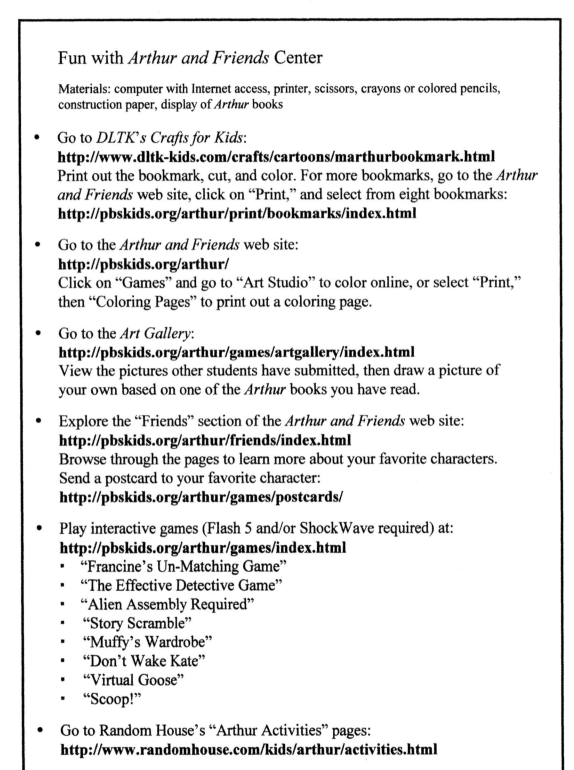

Fun with *Arthur and Friends* Center

Materials: computer with Internet access, printer, scissors, crayons or colored pencils, construction paper, display of *Arthur* books

- Go to *DLTK's Crafts for Kids*:
  http://www.dltk-kids.com/crafts/cartoons/marthurbookmark.html
  Print out the bookmark, cut, and color. For more bookmarks, go to the *Arthur and Friends* web site, click on "Print," and select from eight bookmarks:
  http://pbskids.org/arthur/print/bookmarks/index.html

- Go to the *Arthur and Friends* web site:
  http://pbskids.org/arthur/
  Click on "Games" and go to "Art Studio" to color online, or select "Print," then "Coloring Pages" to print out a coloring page.

- Go to the *Art Gallery*:
  http://pbskids.org/arthur/games/artgallery/index.html
  View the pictures other students have submitted, then draw a picture of your own based on one of the *Arthur* books you have read.

- Explore the "Friends" section of the *Arthur and Friends* web site:
  http://pbskids.org/arthur/friends/index.html
  Browse through the pages to learn more about your favorite characters.
  Send a postcard to your favorite character:
  http://pbskids.org/arthur/games/postcards/

- Play interactive games (Flash 5 and/or ShockWave required) at:
  http://pbskids.org/arthur/games/index.html
  - "Francine's Un-Matching Game"
  - "The Effective Detective Game"
  - "Alien Assembly Required"
  - "Story Scramble"
  - "Muffy's Wardrobe"
  - "Don't Wake Kate"
  - "Virtual Goose"
  - "Scoop!"

- Go to Random House's "Arthur Activities" pages:
  http://www.randomhouse.com/kids/arthur/activities.html

The Eric Carle Web Site

Welcome to the Official Eric Carle Web Site

http://www.eric-carle.com/

Description of Site

The very hungry caterpillar creeps along the top of the home page to welcome visitors to the web site. Once at the site, one can find a biography of the author/illustrator along with an extensive annotated bibliography of his works. There is also an online newsletter called *The Caterpillar Express* which is archived and may be accessed from the *Answers to Frequently Asked Questions* page. There is a link to the web site of the Eric Carle Museum of Picture Book Art (http://www.picturebookart.org/), located in Amherst, Massachusetts. According to the museum's founders, it is "the first full-scale museum in this country devoted to international picture book art, conceived and built with the aim of celebrating the art that we are first exposed to as children and that we carry with us throughout our lives." This web site is a must-see for fans of Eric Carle. Read more about the museum at http://www.eduplace.com/rdg/gen_act/insect/b_fly.html.

Best of Site: Caterpillar Exchange

This section of the web site is for teachers, day care providers, school media specialists, children's librarians, scholars, and parents. It is an e-bulletin board where educators and caregivers using Eric Carle's books in creative ways can submit their ideas. Dozens of Mr. Carle's book titles are linked to suggestions for extending the stories in the classroom or home. At the bottom of each page, Mr. Carle welcomes online submissions. There are literally dozens of activities for most of the titles.

Lesson plan ideas in this chapter...	Special features of site...
◆ *The Very Hungry Caterpillar*	◆ Biography and FAQ's
◆ *The Grouchy Ladybug*	◆ The Eric Carle Museum
◆ *A House for Hermit Crab*	◆ The *Caterpillar Express* Newsletter

About the Author

Eric Carle was born in Syracuse, New York. His parents were German immigrants who moved back to Germany when Eric was six years old. Mr. Carle found German schools to be quite different from American schools in that they observed stricter discipline. This atmosphere played a role in Mr. Carle's philosophy towards young children. He believes that children should have their needs met and that they should be treated with compassion as they grow and develop. He wants to help children adapt more easily to the transition of starting school for the first time. He believes that children should experience delight in literature. Even though Mr. Carle's childhood years in Germany were not always happy, they did have an effect on his future writings. Mr. Carle remembers his walks through gardens and woods with his father. His father would point out the little creatures that lived in these habitats. These walks led to Mr. Carle's love of nature and especially his love of insects. Mr. Carle has a unique style of illustrating which has become his trademark. He uses cut and torn tissue paper and texturizes it with brightly colored acrylic paints to create collages. Mr. Carle has become legendary in the world of children's picture books and has written and illustrated over sixty books.

Online Author Studies

- "Biographical Notes for Eric Carle," *The Official Eric Carle Web Site*, http://www.eric-carle.com/bio.html (25 May 2003).
  This interesting biography on the author's web site shares information about Eric Carle's life, his art, and how he got started writing and illustrating picture books. Click on *The Art of Eric Carle* for an annotated bibliography of his works. Go to the home page and click on *Answers to Frequently Asked Questions* to read more about the author and his work.

- Carpenter, Kathleen Alape. "The Very Busy Museum: A Conversation with Eric Carle," *Teachers.net Gazette*, http://teachers.net/gazette/DEC02/covera.html (25 May 2003).
  This extensive interview will enlighten fans about Eric Carle and his works.

- Carroll, Lee, Piece, Sarre, and Sheerin. "Hastings Kindergarteners Celebrate Eric Carle," *Maria Hastings Elementary School, Lexington, MA*, http://hastings.ci.lexington.ma.us/projects/carle/ (25 May 2003).
  This excellent site contains links to projects and activities relating to Eric Carle and his works. There are photographs to view and examples of students' work.

- "Eric Carle," *Children's Book Council*, http://www.cbcbooks.org/html/ericcarle.html (24 May 2003).
  This site has information about Mr. Carle's love of insects and his early life.

- Hurst, Carol. "Featured Author: Eric Carle," *Carolhurst.com*, http://www.carolhurst.com/newsletters/24dnewsletters.html (May 24 2003).
  This renowned web site, *Carol Hurst's Children's Literature Site*, has a biography, an annotated bibliography, and an essay on Mr. Carle's artwork.

- Kroin, Amy. "The Very Amazing Eric Carle," *Valley Advocate*, http://www.valleyadvocate.com/gbase/Arts/content.html?oid=oid:658 (25 May 2003).
  This site gives details about Eric Carle's life, his works, and the Eric Carle Museum of Picture Book Art.

- "Meet the Writers: Eric Carle," *Barnesandnoble.com*, http://www.barnesandnoble.com/writers/writer.asp?cid=931779 (24 May 2003).
  A detailed biography and interview accompany a brief fact file about the author.

- Murphy, Susan D. "Teacher Cyberguide: The Very Hungry Caterpillar," *Schools of California Online Resources for Educators (SCORE) Project, San Diego County Office of Education*, http://www.sdcoe.k12.ca.us/score/carle/carletg.html (24 May 2003).
  This unit consists of three activities in which students explore these questions:
  1. Who is Eric Carle and where does he live?
  2. Where does he get the ideas for his books?
  3. How does he create his illustrations?
  The site contains links to help students find the answers. As a culminating classroom project, students write and illustrate their own stories using Eric Carle's artwork techniques.

- Rouleau, Sandy and Wendy Buchberg. "Eric Carle Author Study," *Scholastic, Inc.*, http://teacher.scholastic.com/lessonrepro/lessonplans/ecarle.htm (May 24, 2003).
  This extensive author study covers Mr. Carle's early years and how he became an accomplished author/illustrator. It has an interview with the author and contains an annotated bibliography. The author study has details about Mr. Carle's artwork and methods of illustration. It concludes with suggestions for how to use the books in an integrated curriculum and provides lesson ideas.

Eric Carle

Lesson Plan Ideas

The Very Hungry Caterpillar

> Annotation: The story of a caterpillar progressing through the stages of becoming a butterfly. [Putnam Publishing Company, 1971, hardcover ISBN: 0399208534]

- Alexander, Betty. "TeacherView: The Very Hungry Caterpillar," *Education Place, Houghton Mifflin Company,* http://www.eduplace.com/tview/pages/v/The_Very_Hungry_ Caterpillar_Eric_Carle.html (24 May 2003).
This lesson has students research butterflies and write observations in journals.

- Bishop, Elaine and Cindi Kaiser. "Monarch Butterflies," *Teachers.net,* http://www.teachers.net/lessons/posts//393.html (25 May 2003).
This lesson successfully integrates science with literature.

- "Book Plan: The Very Hungry Caterpillar," *Library Media Education Department, Minnesota State University, Mankato,* http://online.coled.mankato.msus.edu/dept/ci/matz/rdgwld/Books/Hungry%20 Caterpillar.html (31 May 2003).
This lesson teaches adjectives, ordinal numbers, art, symmetry, and measurement.

- Bruner, Carrie. "Thematic Unit: Eric Carle's The Very Hungry Caterpillar," http://members.aol.com/cbruner1/ (24 May 2003).
This integrated lesson plan engages students while completing a variety of activities to extend the book. Photographs enhance the presentation of the activities.

- Chapman, Beth Inskeep. "The Very Hungry Caterpillar Sequencing Activity," *Collaborative Lesson Archive, University of Illinois,* http://faldo.atmos.uiuc.edu/CLA/LESSONS/111.html (25 May 2003).
This lesson plan successfully reinforces skills in sequential order, days of the week, vocabulary words for foods, oral language, and writing.

- Hauscarriague, Annette. "Teaching Nutrition Through the Use of Eric Carle's The Very Hungry Caterpillar," *HealthyKids,* http://www.etc.sccoe.k12.ca.us/ i98/ii98Units/Health/healthyk/text/hungry.html (26 May 2003).

This lesson plan teaches the importance of the fruit items found in the story. It has a link to the *Dole 5-A-Day* site for more activities. Use with *DLTK's* "Book Breaks: The Very Hungry Caterpillar" for activities and crafts with fruit: http://www.dltk-teach.com/books/hungrycaterpillar/index.htm.

- Hoyler, Laura. "TeacherView: The Very Hungry Caterpillar," *Education Place, Houghton Mifflin Company*, http://www.eduplace.com/tview/pages/v/The_Very_Hungry_ Caterpillar_Eric_Carle.html (24 May 2003).
  Scroll down the page to see this lesson idea for creating a "wall story" or mural.

- "A Quest with the Hungry Caterpillar," *Happyvale School District #73, British Columbia*, http://happyvale.sd73.bc.ca/quest%20caterpillar.htm (25 May 2003).
  This is an excellent webquest to use after reading the book.

- Smolkin, Laura. "The Very Hungry Caterpillar," *Webbing Into Literacy: A Book a Week*, http://curry.edschool.virginia.edu/go/wil/Caterpillar_Lesson.pdf (26 May 2003).
  This lesson teaches the names of fruit, days of the week, and numbers.

- Van Velzen, Kathy. "The Very Hungry Caterpillar Bulletin Board," *Lucy Siegrist School, San Bernadino County Schools*, http://www.sbcss.k12.ca.us/sbcss/specialeducation/ecthematic/insects/bbi.htm (25 May 2003).
  Get bulletin board ideas from this site. Click on the links for even more pictures.

- "The Very Hungry Caterpillar Unit," *TeachingHeart.net*, http://www.teachingheart.net/veryhungrycaterpillar.html (26 May 2003).
  This is a multi-disciplinary unit with good lessons to use with the story.

The Very Hungry Caterpillar Lesson Enhancements

- *DLTK's* "The Very Hungry Caterpillar Story Sequencing Cards": **http://www.dltk-teach.com/books/hungrycaterpillar/sequencing.htm**
- Food items found in *The Very Hungry Caterpillar*: **http://edtech.kennesaw.edu/traci/insects/food.htm**
- *DLTK's* "The Very Hungry Caterpillar's Felt Board Fun (or Puppets)": **http://www.dltk-teach.com/books/hungrycaterpillar/felt_fun.htm**
- *Allrecipes.com* has an easy cooking activity to use with the story: **http://cakerecipe.com/az/CaterpillarCake.asp**
- "Caterpillars, Butterflies," *CanTeach Songs and Poems*, **http://www.canteach.ca/elementary/songspoems26.html**

The Grouchy Ladybug

> Annotation: The story of an unpleasant ladybug who learns the hard way that using good manners and being happy is the best way to live and get along with others. [HarperCollins, 1977, hardcover ISBN: 006027087X]

- Anderson, Christina, editor. "Linking Technology and Literacy: Grouchy Ladybug," *Madison Metropolitan School District, FL,*
  http://www.madison.k12.fl.us/tnl/langarts/techlit/ladybug.htm (14 June 2003).
  This lesson effectively incorporates word processing skills as students practice using quotation marks to indicate dialogue.

- Blackwell, Vicki. "The Grouchy Ladybug," *Tangipahoa Parish Schools, LA,*
  http://www.vickiblackwell.com/lit/ladybug.html (25 May 2003).
  This site offers multiple technology-related activities to use with the book. There are downloads for bookmarks, labels, glyphs, a unit on feelings, a ladybug clock, and an accordion book. There are also dozens of links to sites about ladybugs.

- Frey, Carol, Roseann Meinholz, and Marcia Reed. "A Quest for Respect with the Grouchy Ladybug," *Yorkville School District #115, IL,*
  http://www.yorkville.k12.il.us/webquests/webqfrey/webqsfrey.html
  (24 May 2003).
  This webquest is a good extension for the book. It includes activities to learn facts about ladybugs, deals with the issue of respect, and provides practice in making a time chart. Two rubrics are included with the webquest.

- Seagraves, S. "Ladybugs," *Mrs. Seagraves' QUEST Class Pages,*
  http://www.geocities.com/Athens/Atrium/5924/schoolyardscience.htm
  (24 May 2003).
  This well-done site has many ideas for teachers to use as curriculum tie-ins with the book including *Ladybug Facts*, *Ladybug Games*, *Ladybug Crafts*, and *Ladybug Photos*. From the *Teacher's Guide*, one can access the *Ladybug Life Cycle Worksheet* (Adobe Acrobat required). The site also has links to other sites about ladybugs.

A House for Hermit Crab

> Annotation: A hermit crab outgrows his shell and moves into a new one while getting to know the neighboring sea creatures. [Simon & Schuster, 1991, hardcover ISBN: 0887081681]

- Abbuhl, Ann, Laura Carlson, Pat Dobson, and Yvonne Kenyon. "Hermit Crabs WebQuest,"
  http://projects.edtech.sandi.net/sessions/hermitcrab/hermitcrabtchr.html
  (28 September 2003).

This webquest offers a good framework for the study of hermit crabs to extend the story. There are, however, several links that do not work. Click on *Hermit Crab Research Sheet* to print a worksheet for students to use. Click on *Bobo the Hermit Crab* link to read about a pet hermit crab owned by Oliver Braun. Click on *Rubric* to see how the webquest can be evaluated.

- Espiritu, Margarita M. "The Hermit Crab: a Crabby House Hunter," *Lessons.ph Web Magazine*, http://www.lessons.ph/webmag/ish006/personality.shtml
  (30 June 2003).

This is a good article to learn factual information about the hermit crab.

- Garcia, Patrick and Linda Lungren. "Designing Hermit's New Home WebQuest,"
  http://projects.edtech.sandi.net/valencia/puppetplay/ (25 May 2003).

This is an excellent webquest to learn about hermit crabs and their habits. To get started, click on *Introduction* from the main menu. There are many links to help students through the task assignment and process. There is also a rubric.

- "A House for Hermit Crab," *North Carolina National Estuarine Research Reserve Education Office*,
  http://www.ncnerr.org/education/lessons/hermitcrab/hermit_crab.html
  (30 June 2003).

This lesson plan has good activities to learn about the hermit crab and its habitat.

- Treasures at Sea. "A House for Hermit Crab," *Franklin Institute Online*,
  http://www.fi.edu/fellows/fellow8/dec98/crab.html (25 May 2003).

This is an excellent site to learn about hermit crabs after reading the story. There are several hyperlinks to expand the lesson into center activities. Click on *Maze* for an online maze activity. Click on *Animals* for an interactive word search for sea animals that live in the intertidal zone (a Java-enabled browser is required). Click on *Rebus Story* to read and then have students create their own rebus stories using *KidPix*, *Kidspiration*, or *KidWorks*.

Classroom Center Ideas

Collage Art Center

Materials: display of Eric Carle's books, tissue paper, brightly colored acrylic paints, paintbrushes in various sizes, scissors, glue, construction paper, black markers, computer with Internet access, printer, teacher-created example of a collage

Prior to going to the centers, model how tissue paper collages are made. Instruct the class on techniques and discuss each step in the process. Make an example for students to examine. Have students study the illustrations in Mr. Carle's books. After studying the examples of collage, students will choose an animal and create a collage in the style of Eric Carle.

- *Storyopolis*:
  http://www.storyopolis.com/portfolio-dbp.asp?ArtistID=123
  Use this site to enlarge and view the front covers of many of Mr. Carle's books to see his art techniques.

- *2nd Grade Collages*:
  This is a Maryland school's web site showing Mrs. Bermudez's student-created collages (under the direction of student teacher, Mrs. Cantorna): **http://www.mcps.k12.md.us/schools/forestknollses/studentwork/collage.htm**

- *Student Art Inspired by Eric Carle*:
  http://www.pausd.palo-alto.ca.us/hays/artstudio/carle_art.html
  This site contains outstanding examples of collages made by students in the style of Eric Carle. Click on *Making the Art* to link to instructions. Click on *Student Descriptions of Lessons and Techniques* to read students' comments and explanations about the process of making collages.

- *Peter Waxler's "Eric Carle is Awesome"* at
  http://www.ga.k12.pa.us/academics/ls/K/authors/ericcarle/index.htm
  Click on *Animal Stories: Our Homage to Eric Carle* to see collages by students at Germantown Academy in Fort Washington, PA.

- *Maria Hastings School, Lexington, MA*:
  http://hastings.ci.lexington.ma.us/projects/carle/art.html
  View students' collages in the style of Eric Carle.

- *Vivian Redfern's "Very Hungry Caterpillar: Tissue Collage"* at
  http://www.kinderart.com/across/cater.shtml
  This step-by-step lesson makes it look easy to create collages.

Caterpillar and Butterfly Craft Center

Materials: computer with Internet access, printer, crayons or colored pencils, scissors, glue

- Coloring pages:
  The Environmental Protection Agency's Endangered Species Coloring Book
  to color a captioned butterfly picture:
  http://www.lacoast.gov/kids/coloringbooks/endangered/butterfly.htm

  Leanne's Butterfly Themed Coloring Pages:
  http://www.coloring.ws/butterfly1.htm

  PrimaryGames.com for coloring pages that include the life cycle:
  http://www.primarygames.com/science/butterflies/coloring.htm

- Need a butterfly or caterpillar pattern?
  Science Museum of Minnesota:
  http://www.sci.mus.mn.us/sln/tf/s/symmetry/butterflypattern.gif

  Sassy's coloring page:
  http://www.geocities.com/Heartland/Plains/7316/coloringpages/color17.htm

  Journey North's pattern from *Learner.org*:
  http://www.learner.org/jnorth/www/jsouth/templ1.html

  Activity Village's Summer Butterflies site for three mobile patterns:
  http://www.activityvillage.co.uk/summer_butterflies.htm

  Western Exterminator:
  http://www.westernexterminator.com/fun_butterfly.html

  University of Minnesota's Monarchs in the Classroom site for a caterpillar
  pattern: **http://www.sci.mus.mn.us/sln/tf/n/nowyouseeit/cat2.gif**

- Coffee filter butterflies:
  Kids Domain Craft Exchange:
  http://www.lacoast.gov/kids/coloringbooks/endangered/butterfly.htm

  Karen LaVarnway's "Tissue Paper Butterflies" at *KinderArt*:
  http://kinderart.com/painting/tissuebutterfly.shtml
  View step-by-step, illustrated directions from Ms. Hines' class at Jack
  Hulland Elementary School.

More Craft Center Ideas

- *Enchanted Learning's* "Butterfly and Caterpillar Crafts":
  http://www.enchantedlearning.com/crafts/butterfly/
  and **http://www.enchantedlearning.com/subjects/butterfly/**
  Select from over a dozen illustrated craft activities.

- Stained glass butterflies:
  Yukon Butterflies activity site:
  http://www.yesnet.yk.ca/schools/jackhulland/projects/butterflies/

  Houghton Mifflin's Beautiful Butterflies:
  http://www.eduplace.com/rdg/gen_act/insect/b_fly.html

- Peggy Goldman's "Art Fun Twists Butterfly" at *ClassroomDirect.com*:
  http://familyeducation.com/article/0,1120,8-13746,00.html
  This is an eye-catching butterfly that students will have fun making.

- Butterfly patterns to color, a butterfly lace-up card, and butterfly stick
  puppets at *Treasures of the Heart*:
  http://www.geocities.com/treasureschildcare/colorsheets/b.html

- J. R. William's "Egg Carton Caterpillar" at *KinderArt*:
  http://kinderart.com/across/eggcaterpillar.shtml
  After making the caterpillar, students wait fourteen days and make an
  emerging butterfly.

- Trish Wade's "The Very Hungry Caterpillar" lesson at *KinderArt*:
  http://kinderart.com/across/hungrycat.shtml
  This art activity reinforces sequencing, counting, days of the week, and the
  life cycle of a butterfly.

Butterfly Life Cycle Center

Materials: computer with Internet access, printer, crayons or colored pencils, scissors, glue

- *Enchanted Learning's Butterfly* pages:
  http://www.enchantedlearning.com/subjects/butterfly/
  Click on *All About Butterflies*, *Life Cycle*, *Anatomy*, *Illustrated Dictionary*, and *Web Links* to research butterflies. Click on *Printouts* to get life cycle labeling activities, a Venn diagram, and sequencing cards.

- The *U.S. Geological Survey's* "The Children's Butterfly Site":
  http://www.mesc.nbs.gov/resources/education/butterfly/bfly_start.asp
  Visit for enlargeable drawings of the life cycle of a butterfly, a gallery of butterfly photographs, and an activity on raising caterpillars.

- *Michael Hogan's Butterflies of the Pine Barrens*:
  http://www.hoganphoto.com/butterflies.htm
  Select from beautiful photographs to view butterflies in various stages.

- The *Scotia-Glenville Children's Museum's* "Where do Butterflies Come From?": **http://www.hhmi.org/coolscience/butterfly/**
  See the life cycle art activity and butterfly life cycle animation.
  For another life cycle activity, go to *Bry-BackManor.org's* site:
  http://www.bry-backmanor.org/actpag36.html

- David A. McClung's "Emergence of a Monarch" at the *Welcome To The Florida Monarch Butterfly Website*:
  http://adver-net.com/Monemerg.html
  View outstanding photographs with captions of the butterfly life cycle.

- *Butterflies North and South* has a virtual butterfly life cycle exhibit:
  http://www.virtualmuseum.ca/Exhibitions/Butterflies/english/teach+games/index.html

- Jenna Dower's "Caterpillar to Butterfly" at the *Science Museum of Minnesota* site:
  http://butterflywebsite.com/articles/ShowArticle.cfm?ID=483
  This well done slide show effectively demonstrates a student-created multimedia presentation. After viewing, students can draft a storyboard and create slide shows using presentation software such as mPower.

Caterpillar and Butterfly Activity Center

Materials: computer with Internet access, printer, crayons or colored pencils

- Interactive Online Activities:
  Houghton Mifflin's Build a Story: **http://www.eduplace.com/cgi-bin/hmr-build-a-story.cgi?ID=/story/butterfly&START_STORY=1**

  Scholastic's Build Your Own Caterpillar:
  http://teacher.scholastic.com/activities/explorer/ecosystems/be_an_explorer/map/caterpillar_play.htm

  The Butterfly Pavilion's Hide and Seek activity:
  http://www.butterflies.org/hidenseek.htm

  Yukon Butterflies for seven fun butterfly games:
  http://www.yesnet.yk.ca/schools/jackhulland/projects/butterflies/

- *Munchinland's Calvin Caterpillar Likes the Letter C*:
  Find this phonics worksheet at
  http://www.geocities.com/athens/delphi/7844/caterpillar.html

- Read and listen to *KidzClub.com's* online story, *I Wish,* about a caterpillar wishing he could fly:
  http://www.kizclub.com/storytime/caterpillar/caterpillar1.html

- *Enchanted Learning's* "Math Coloring Activity":
  http://www.allaboutbutterflies.com/subjects/butterfly/
  This is an excellent butterfly math activity to reinforce addition skills.

- *Enchanted Learning's Zoom Butterfly* pages:
  http://www.enchantedlearning.com/subjects/butterfly/
  Click on *Classroom Activities* and select from dozens of puzzles, printouts, a cloze activity, a calendar, a butterfly book, butterfly math, and quizzes.

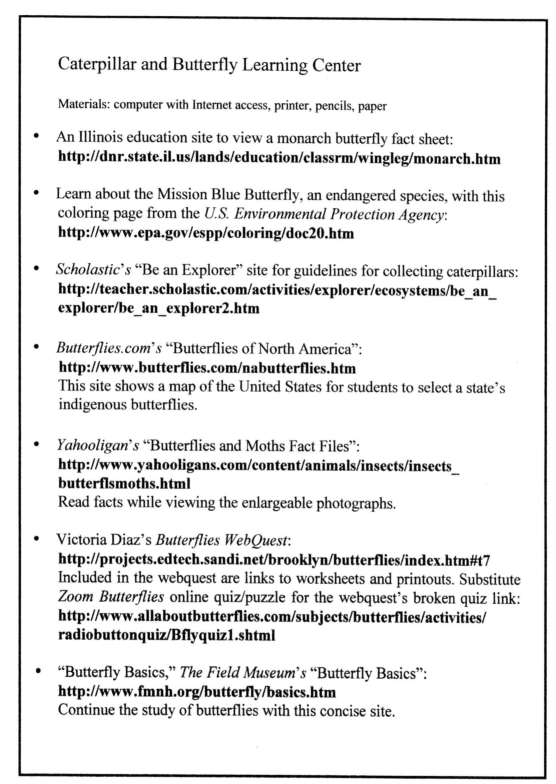

Caterpillar and Butterfly Learning Center

Materials: computer with Internet access, printer, pencils, paper

- An Illinois education site to view a monarch butterfly fact sheet: **http://dnr.state.il.us/lands/education/classrm/wingleg/monarch.htm**

- Learn about the Mission Blue Butterfly, an endangered species, with this coloring page from the *U.S. Environmental Protection Agency*: **http://www.epa.gov/espp/coloring/doc20.htm**

- *Scholastic's* "Be an Explorer" site for guidelines for collecting caterpillars: **http://teacher.scholastic.com/activities/explorer/ecosystems/be_an_ explorer/be_an_explorer2.htm**

- *Butterflies.com's* "Butterflies of North America": **http://www.butterflies.com/nabutterflies.htm** This site shows a map of the United States for students to select a state's indigenous butterflies.

- *Yahooligan's* "Butterflies and Moths Fact Files": **http://www.yahooligans.com/content/animals/insects/insects_ butterflsmoths.html** Read facts while viewing the enlargeable photographs.

- Victoria Diaz's *Butterflies WebQuest*: **http://projects.edtech.sandi.net/brooklyn/butterflies/index.htm#t7** Included in the webquest are links to worksheets and printouts. Substitute *Zoom Butterflies* online quiz/puzzle for the webquest's broken quiz link: **http://www.allaboutbutterflies.com/subjects/butterflies/activities/ radiobuttonquiz/Bflyquiz1.shtml**

- "Butterfly Basics," *The Field Museum's* "Butterfly Basics": **http://www.fmnh.org/butterfly/basics.htm** Continue the study of butterflies with this concise site.

Ladybug Center

Materials: computer with Internet access, printer, crayons or colored pencils, discarded CDs or CD-ROMs, glue, red, white, and black construction paper, scissors, pencils

- Ladybug coloring and labeling pages at *Enchanted Learning*:
  http://www.enchantedlearning.com/subjects/insects/Ladybug.shtml

- *DLTK's* "Printable Crafts for Kids":
  http://www.dltk-kids.com/rhymes/ladybug_cd_rom_craft.htm
  Print the template provided on the site and follow the instructions to make this imaginative ladybug from an old CD or CD-ROM.

- *DLTK's* "Ladybug, Ladybug Coloring Book":
  http://www.coloring.ws/ladybugs1.htm
  This site has a variety of enlargeable black and white pages to color.

- *DLTK's* "L is for Ladybug Tracer Pages":
  http://www.dltk-kids.com/rhymes/mladybugtracer.html
  This tracing page can be used to reinforce manuscript handwriting skills and the sound of the letter "L".

- *DLTK's* "Ladybug, Ladybug Finger Puppets":
  http://www.dltk-kids.com/rhymes/mladybugfinger.html
  Students will have fun making these finger puppets.

- *DLTK's* "Ladybug Egg Carton Craft":
  http://www.dltk-kids.com/crafts/insects/ladybug_egg_carton_craft.htm
  This is a good craft idea to make a 3-D ladybug.

- *Enchanted Learning's* printouts:
  http://www.enchantedlearning.com/subjects/insects/Ladybug.shtml
  Select from a coloring page and a life cycle labeling page.

- *Illinois Department of Natural Resources* fact sheet with diagram:
  http://dnr.state.il.us/lands/education/classrm/wingleg/ladybug.htm

- *Treasures of the Heart* for a ladybug coloring sheet:
  http://www.geocities.com/treasureschildcare/colorsheets/ladybugs.html

- *Jerri's Ladybug Links*:
  http://webtech.kennesaw.edu/jcheek3/ladybugs.htm

© Permissions

All images on the Eric Carle web site are copyright protected and may not be downloaded or copied.

⊠ Making Contact

E-mail:
ideas@eric-carle.com

Write to:
Eric Carle
P.O. Box 485
Northampton, MA 01060

The Denise Fleming Web Site

Welcome to My Website

http://www.denisefleming.com

Description of Site

The author's web site is a dazzling array of bright colors and illustrations in the style that has become her trademark. The site captivates one's attention and is sure to be a hit with kids. The author has placed activities for each of her books on the site. She also has posted a biography, photographs, an interview, and a colorful, illustrated bibliography of her books with annotations and reviews. This site is particularly interesting because it contains detailed information about papermaking and pulp painting.

Best of Site: Papermaking Instructions

Papermaking and pulp painting are the author's preferred media. She gives detailed information about this craft and has also posted three sets of instructions for papermaking activities in the classroom: papermaking, making a handmade journal, and making handmade paper from t-paper. All of these instructions are in pdf format and require Adobe Acrobat. This topic would lend itself well to learning more about the history of papermaking through the ages. See also the Baltimore County Public Library's site for Denise Fleming's instructions for bookbinding:
http://www.bcpl.info/kidspage/kids_flem_bookbinding.html (27 April 2003).

Lesson plan ideas in this chapter...	Special features of site...
◆ *Where Once There Was a Wood* ◆ *Lunch* ◆ *In the Small, Small Pond*	◆ Book Activities ◆ Link to the *Mazza Collection*: Virtual Tour of Picture Book Art

About the Author

Denise Fleming learned to experiment with arts and crafts at a very young age while she spent time with her furniture-making father in the family's basement. She loved to read and work with papier-mache and wood. She won several awards for art in high school and went on to attend the Kendall College of Art and Design in Grand Rapids, Michigan. After meeting her husband and becoming a mother, she became enamored with children's picture books. She realized that she would like to create picture books and went on to write and illustrate her first book, *In the Tall, Tall Grass* in 1991. In 1994 she produced a companion book entitled *In the Small, Small Pond* which received a Caldecott Honor Award. Ms. Fleming's books are works of art and are especially loved by children and early childhood educators.

Online Author Studies

- "Denise Fleming," *Baltimore County Public Library*,
    http://www.bcplonline.org/kidspage/fleming.html#Biography (27 April 2003).
  This site has a brief biography about the author/illustrator.

- "Denise Fleming," *Bookworm Enterprises*,
    http://www.friend.ly.net/scoop/biographies/flemingdenise/ (27 April 2003).
  This site has an interview with the author and a link to her booklist.

- "Denise Fleming," *Kidsreads.com*, http://www.kidsreads.com/authors/
    au-fleming-denise.asp (27 April 2003).
  Read what the author has to say about her favorite foods, hobbies, pets, and activities.

- Fleming, Denise. "A Visit with Denise Fleming," *Denisefleming.com*,
    http://denisefleming.com/Pages/Biography.html (30 June 2003).
  This is an autobiography about the author's early years and her interest in the arts.

- Fleming, Denise. "Studio Views: Pulp Painting," March/April 1998, *Horn Book
    Magazine*, http://www.hbook.com/studio_fleming.shtml (27 April 2003).
  Here, the author explains her artistic medium, pulp painting, and papermaking for book illustration.

Lesson Plan Ideas

Where Once There Was a Wood

> Annotation: The book teaches children about the importance of saving natural habitats, what happens to wildlife when their habitats are destroyed, and how to reduce habitat destruction due to development. [Henry Holt and Company, 2000, paperback ISBN: 0805064826]

- "Endangered Species Coloring Book," *U.S. Environmental Protection Agency*, http://www.epa.gov/espp/coloring/ (4 May 2003).
  This activity may be downloaded and printed for students to color as they learn about habitat destruction to wildlife. Prior to coloring, view the site with a video projector and discuss the issue as a whole class activity. Click on the link *Learn About Endangered Species* for more information.

- Khan, Iram. "TeacherView: Where Once There Was a Wood," *The Education Place, Houghton Mifflin Company*, http://www.eduplace.com/tview/tviews/w/whereoncetherewasawood.html (27 April 2003).
   This is a good activity to introduce habitats to children.

- "Why are Forests Being Cleared?" *EcoKids Online*, http://www.ecokidsonline.com/pub/eco_info/topics/forests/forests_being_cleared .cfm (4 May 2003).
  This is an excellent site to explain habitat destruction and its consequences. Use with a video projector as a slide show for whole class viewing.

Lunch

> Annotation: A hungry mouse eats his way through nutritious and colorful fruits and vegetables. [Henry Holt and Company, 1996, paperback ISBN: 0805046461]

- "Let's Read! Lunch," *Texas Department of Health*, http://www.tdh.state.tx.us/kids/lessonplans/chap8_1.htm (3 May 2003).
  This lesson plan provides several activities to use with the book, including a "Lunch Cards" sequencing activity and recipes from the book.

- Smith-Horn, Lisa. "Teaching Adjectives with Denise Fleming's *Lunch*," *AskERIC.org*, http://www.askeric.org/cgi-bin/printlessons.cgi/Virtual/Lessons/Language_Arts/Literature/Childrens_Literature/CHL0216.html (27 April 2003).
  This lesson plan engages students while they learn about adjectives.

In the Small, Small Pond

> Annotation: A pond habitat is showcased with rhyming text as the seasons change from spring to fall and fall to winter. [Henry Holt and Company, 1998, paperback ISBN: 0805059830]

- "Pond Explorer," *Canterbury Environmental Education Centre*, http://www.naturegrid.org.uk/pondexplorer/pondexplorer.html (3 May 2003).
  This comprehensive site contains information about pond life for primary grades. It has many ideas for teachers to use in a lesson about ponds. Activities include a pond investigation, a virtual pond dip, an identification key, an activity sheet, an interactive pond exploration, and notes and links for teachers. Use with a video projector as a whole class activity.

Classroom Center Ideas

Habitat Destruction Center

Materials: computer with Internet access, printer

- Go to the U.S. Environmental Protection Agency's "What's Wrong with this Picture" site:
  http://www.epa.gov/OWOW/NPS/kids/whatwrng.htm
  Students can play an interactive game to see if they can find the ways that people harm the environment.

- "Eco-Storybook," *ExoKids Online*:
  http://www.ecokidsonline.com/pub/fun_n_games/storybook/index.cfm (4 May 2003).
  Choose from four interactive storybooks to read about habitat destruction.

Virtual Pond Center

Materials: computer with Internet access, white construction paper, crayons or colored pencils

- View the following web sites about microorganisms that live in ponds:
  Van Egmond, Wim. "A Virtual Pond Dip," *Microscopy UK*:
  http://www.microscopy-uk.org.uk/ponddip/index.html
  This online activity allows students to click on images in a virtual jar of pond water to learn about small organisms that live in a pond.

  Van Egmond, Wim. "The Smallest Page on the Web," *Microscopy UK*:
  http://www.microscopy-uk.org.uk/mag/wimsmall/small.html
  This site allows students to view excellent images of microscopic organisms that live in a freshwater pond.

- View the following web sites about animals and plants that live in ponds:
  "Aquatic Critters," *Missouri Botanical Garden*:
  http://mbgnet.mobot.org/fresh/slide/index.htm
  Use this slide show to learn about animal and plant life in ponds.
  Excellent photographs accompany the slide show and can be enlarged.

  "Pond," *Sir Robert Hitcham's Primary School, Suffolk, UK*:
  http://www.hitchams.suffolk.sch.uk/habitats/pond.htm
  This is a good introductory site on pond animals for young children.

  "Pond Life Animal Printouts," *EnchantedLearning.com*:
  http://www.enchantedlearning.com/biomes/pond/pondlife.shtml
  This site has good pictures and diagrams of pond animals, a cover sheet for a pond study, which can be colored and printed, and excellent information about each animal.

- Students can complete the *Pond Habitat Chart* (page 49) from the information they learn on the web sites. They will select three or more microorganisms that live in ponds, three or more plants that live in ponds, and three or more animals that live in ponds. They will draw and label pictures of their selections and write one fact about each entry.

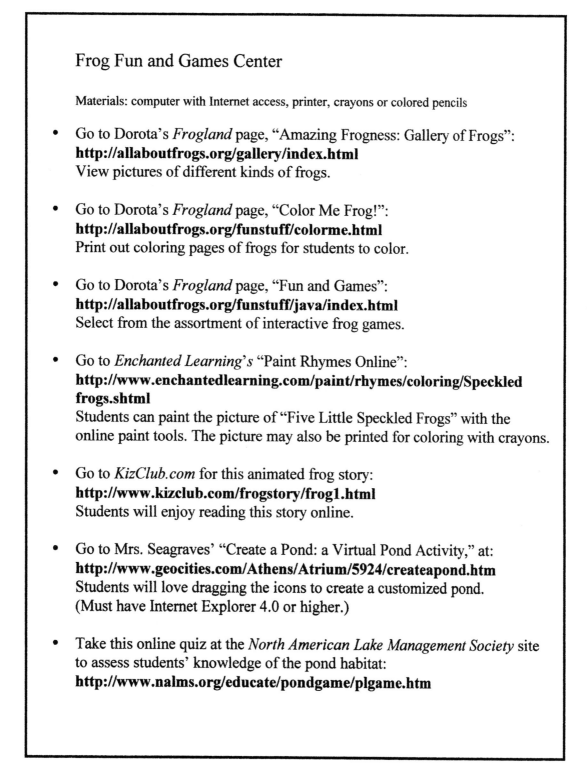

Frog Fun and Games Center

Materials: computer with Internet access, printer, crayons or colored pencils

- Go to Dorota's *Frogland* page, "Amazing Frogness: Gallery of Frogs":
  http://allaboutfrogs.org/gallery/index.html
  View pictures of different kinds of frogs.

- Go to Dorota's *Frogland* page, "Color Me Frog!":
  http://allaboutfrogs.org/funstuff/colorme.html
  Print out coloring pages of frogs for students to color.

- Go to Dorota's *Frogland* page, "Fun and Games":
  http://allaboutfrogs.org/funstuff/java/index.html
  Select from the assortment of interactive frog games.

- Go to *Enchanted Learning's* "Paint Rhymes Online":
  http://www.enchantedlearning.com/paint/rhymes/coloring/Speckled frogs.shtml
  Students can paint the picture of "Five Little Speckled Frogs" with the online paint tools. The picture may also be printed for coloring with crayons.

- Go to *KizClub.com* for this animated frog story:
  http://www.kizclub.com/frogstory/frog1.html
  Students will enjoy reading this story online.

- Go to Mrs. Seagraves' "Create a Pond: a Virtual Pond Activity," at:
  http://www.geocities.com/Athens/Atrium/5924/createapond.htm
  Students will love dragging the icons to create a customized pond.
  (Must have Internet Explorer 4.0 or higher.)

- Take this online quiz at the *North American Lake Management Society* site to assess students' knowledge of the pond habitat:
  http://www.nalms.org/educate/pondgame/plgame.htm

Pond Craft Center

- ## Tadpole Puppet

  Materials: computer with Internet access, green or white construction paper, crayons, fasteners, hole puncher

  1. Go to *Scholastic's* "Tadpole Transformation" web site at: **http://teacher.scholastic.com/lessonrepro/lessonplans/profbooks/ tadpole.pdf**

  2. Print the templates of the body parts shown at the bottom of the page.

  3. Assemble the tadpole then gradually add the body parts needed to make each stage in a frog's metamorphosis.

- ## Frog Puppet

  Materials: red, green, white, and black construction paper, scissors, glue, computer with Internet access, printer, brown paper bag (optional)

  1. Go to *DLTK's* "Circle Fractions Frog Craft" web site: **http://www.dltk-kids.com/animals/mcircle_frog.htm**

  2. Print the circle templates and have students trace the patterns onto construction paper.

  3. Cut out the shapes and assemble to make a frog face. Glue the pieces together.

  4. Optional: Glue the frog face onto a lunch-size brown paper bag to make a puppet.

© Permissions

✉ Making Contact

E-mail the author:
denise@denisefleming.com

Pond Habitat Chart

Name _____

Microorganisms:

Name	Picture	Fact
1. _____		_____
		_____
2. _____		_____
		_____
3. _____		_____
		_____

Animals:

Name	Picture	Fact
1. _____		_____
		_____
2. _____		_____
		_____
3. _____		_____
		_____

Plants:

Name	Picture	Fact
1. _____		_____
		_____
2. _____		_____
		_____
3. _____		_____
		_____

The Kevin Henkes Web Site

Welcome to kevinhenkes.com!

http://www.kevinhenkes.com/young.html

Description of Site

Fans of Kevin Henkes will find pages for his popular mice characters: Wendell, Chrysanthemum, Owen, Sheila Rae, Lilly, Julius, Wemberly, and Chester. Each character's page has activities such as mazes, dot-to-dots, word searches, and coloring pages. Children will delight in these activities after reading the books. Other features of the site are a brief autobiography and an interview with the author, which give insight into his works, his background, and how he gets ideas for his stories. Mr. Henkes is quite prolific as a writer and his site reflects his many other works, which include novels for older children.

Best of Site: The "Mice" Character Pages

Click on the icon for each of the renowned mice characters to access their pages. The information on the pages introduces the characters and gives insight into their personalities and unique qualities. Off to the side of each of the pages, there is a trivia question that will delight students and challenge them to go back to the story to find the answer. The character pages should be used in conjunction with the *Fun and Games* pages because each character has his/her own set of activities to complete.

Lesson plan ideas in this chapter...	Special features of site...
♦ *Chrysanthemum*	♦ Fun and Games
♦ *Lilly's Purple Plastic Purse*	♦ Wemberly and Lilly Party
♦ *Sheila Rae the Brave*	♦ Character Matching Quiz

About the Author

Kevin Henkes knew he wanted to be an artist at a young age and was encouraged by a high school teacher to combine his artistic talents with his writing talents to create children's picture books. After graduation, he published his first book at the age of nineteen. His works now number in the dozens and fans eagerly await his forthcoming works. Mr. Henkes is the recipient of many awards including the distinguished Caldecott Honor Award for excellence in picture book illustration for the book *Owen*. Mr. Henkes often uses mice as characters in his books. His characters portray common childhood fears, disappointments, issues with siblings and peers, and conflicts. Mr. Henkes is adept at portraying children's feelings about everyday occurrences through his characters. The imaginative resolutions in his stories are surprising and amusing and children will definitely identify with his characters, their problems, and their antics. As an illustrator, Mr. Henkes uses black ink and watercolors to create delicate and detailed illustrations.

Online Author Studies

- Cammack, Bruce. "Exhibits: Kevin Henkes," *National Center for Children's Illustrated Literature*, http:/www.nccil.org/exhibit/henkes.html (1 June 2003).
  This site contains a biography and discusses the author's writing style and illustration techniques. Click on *For Children* to access art activities.

- Cary, Alice. "Special Interview with Author and Illustrator, Kevin Henkes: Lilly's Purple Plastic Purse," *BookPage.com*, http://www.bookpage.com/9609bp/childrens/lillypurpleplasticpurse.html (1 June 2003).
  This interview gives insight into Mr. Henkes' childhood and the inspiration for *Lilly's Purple Plastic Purse*.

- Henkes, Kevin. "Meet Kevin," *Welcome to KevinHenkes.com*, http://www.kevinhenkes.com/ (June 1 2003).
  This biography is from the author's web site.

- Stan, Susan. "Wisconsin Authors and Illustrators: Kevin Henkes," *Cooperative Children's Book Center, School of Education, University of Wisconsin-Madison* (Reprinted from *The Five Owls*, November/December 1991), http://www.soemadison.wisc.edu/ccbc/wisauth/henkes/main.htm (1 June 2003).
  This article discusses Mr. Henkes' childhood passion for art and reading and has a link to an extensive bibliography of journal articles about the author, an awards list, a book list, and a link to other web sites about the author.

Lesson Plan Ideas

Chrysanthemum

> Annotation: The story of a little mouse who loves her beautiful, long, flowery name, Chrysanthemum. That is, until she starts school. Her classmates mercilessly tease her about her name until the music teacher announces the name she wants for her soon-to-be-born baby. [William Morrow and Company, 1996, paperback ISBN: 0688147321]

- "Chrysanthemum," *Linking Technology and Literacy, Madison Metropolitan School District, WI,*
  http://www.madison.k12.wi.us/tnl/langarts/techlit/chrysanthemum.htm
  (1 June 2003).
  This lesson plan utilizes the *Kid Pix* program for students to create pictures of flowers with their name on the flowers. This lesson provides practice with keyboarding skills, working with fonts, and using drawing and painting tools. (Other programs may be substituted.) Take the lesson a step further and have students write a caption for their picture telling about themselves. Display the pictures or make a class book.

- Porter, Traci, Cindy Stevens, and Heidi Weber. "TeacherViews: Chrysanthemum," *Education Place, Houghton Mifflin Company,*
  http://www.eduplace.com/tview/pages/c/Chrysanthemum_Kevin_Henkes.html
  (1 June 2003).
  This set of three lesson plans can be used for first day/week of school activities. Included are activities with graphs, classifying, making a class name book, learning the history of names, handwriting, a gardening activity, and making a sand art desk nameplate.

- Tokunaga, Christine K., Eulalia Castelo, and J. C. Rodriguez. "Chrysanthemum: What's in a Name?" *Cesar Chavez Elementary School, San Diego Unified School District,* http://projects.edtech.sandi.net/chavez/Chrysanthemum/top.htm
  (14 June 2003).
  This well-organized webquest, in both English and Spanish, incorporates an author study and individual activities for six of Kevin Henkes' books. Linked to the webquest are a *Kevin Henkes Graphic Organizer* and an *Evaluation Sheet.*

Sheila Rae, the Brave

> Annotation: Sheila Rae prides herself on not being afraid of things that most children are afraid of: the dark, thunderstorms, monsters under the bed, big scary dogs, etc. She thinks her sister, Louise, is a "scaredy cat." [HarperCollins Children's Books, 1987, hardcover ISBN: 0688071554]

- Alexander, Betty. "TeacherView: Sheila Rae, the Brave," *Education Place, Houghton Mifflin Company,*
  http://www.eduplace.com/tview/tviews/s/sheilaraethebrave.html (1 June 2003).
This lesson idea addresses common feelings, such as anger, happiness, sadness, disappointment, pride, embarrassment, fear, and confusion.

Lilly's Purple Plastic Purse

> Annotation: Lilly's grandmother buys her some delightful gifts that she simply must show her classmates at school. Unfortunately, she shows them during inappropriate times, causing disruptions during lessons and storytimes. Lilly gets angry with her teacher, Mr. Slinger, for taking away her treasures. [William Morrow and Company, 1996, hardcover ISBN: 068812898X]

- "Curricula, Lessons, and Activities: Lilly's Purple Plastic Purse," *The Kennedy Center ArtsEdge,* http://artsedge.kennedycenter.org/teaching_materials/curricula/ curriculum_units.dfm?curriculum_ (1 June 2003).
This unit plan contains five individual lesson plans for the book. The lesson themes include bike safety, the color purple, and coins. This unit supports the Kennedy Center production of *Lilly's Purple Plastic Purse.* Visit the Kennedy Center web site at http://www.kennedy-center.org/programs/family/lilly. Read interviews with the cast, read about the lighting, costumes, sound, and sets, and information about the author and playwright.

- H. Traci, M. Velez, and Anita Wilfong. "Lilly's Purple Plastic Purse," *ProTeacher BusyBoard Community,* http://www.proteacher.net/dcforum/busy_board/3002.html (1 June 2003).
Select from three ideas to use with the book. Ideas include math activities, vocabulary words, writing prompts, a money activity, and character education activities.

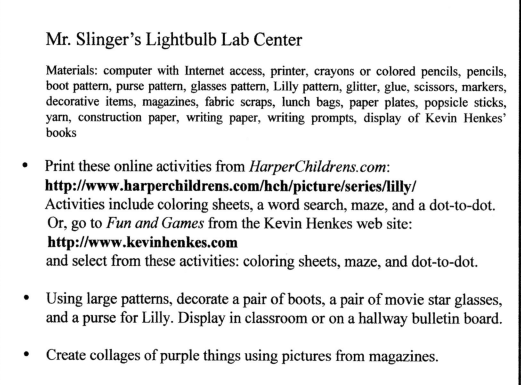

Mr. Slinger's Lightbulb Lab Center

Materials: computer with Internet access, printer, crayons or colored pencils, pencils, boot pattern, purse pattern, glasses pattern, Lilly pattern, glitter, glue, scissors, markers, decorative items, magazines, fabric scraps, lunch bags, paper plates, popsicle sticks, yarn, construction paper, writing paper, writing prompts, display of Kevin Henkes' books

- Print these online activities from *HarperChildrens.com*:
  http://www.harperchildrens.com/hch/picture/series/lilly/
  Activities include coloring sheets, a word search, maze, and a dot-to-dot.
  Or, go to *Fun and Games* from the Kevin Henkes web site:
  http://www.kevinhenkes.com
  and select from these activities: coloring sheets, maze, and dot-to-dot.

- Using large patterns, decorate a pair of boots, a pair of movie star glasses, and a purse for Lilly. Display in classroom or on a hallway bulletin board.

- Create collages of purple things using pictures from magazines.

- Create a puppet play for one of Kevin Henkes' mice stories.

© Permissions

✉ Making Contact

Write to:
Kevin Henkes c/o Greenwillow Books
1350 Avenue of the Americas
New York, NY 10019

Story Elements Activity

Student Name _____

Identify the following elements after reading a book by Kevin Henkes:

Title _____

Author _____

Publisher _____

Place of Publication _____ Copyright Date _____

Characters _____

_____

_____

Setting _____

Problem _____

_____

_____

Solution _____

_____

_____

Review_____

_____

The William Joyce Web Sites

The World of William Joyce
http://www.harperchildrens.com/williamjoyce/homepage.htm

Meet the Author: William Joyce
http://www.harperchildrens.com/hch/author/author/joyce/

Description of Sites

There are actually two web sites for William Joyce, and both are part of *HarperChildrens.com*. The first site, *The World of William Joyce*, has ample biographical material and a lengthy question and answer interview with the author. Mr. Joyce explains how he gets ideas for his books, how he illustrates his books, and childhood experiences that helped influence his writing and art. The site offers coloring pages for two of Mr. Joyce's books, *The Leaf Men and the Brave Good Bugs* and *Bently and Egg*. The second web site, *Meet the Author: William Joyce*, offers good information on each of Mr. Joyce's books, including reviews, awards, and enlargeable illustrations and excerpts. One of Mr. Joyce's books, *Rolie Polie Olie*, has special pages within the site and offers additional activities.

Best of Site: Illustrations and Book Excerpts

The *Meet the Author: William Joyce* web site has a feature that will help students learn about picture book illustration by examining enlargements of the book pages. This feature can also give teachers a useful tool to teach illustration mediums. This section of the web site can be found by clicking on each of the titles listed in Mr. Joyce's book list.

Lesson plan ideas in this chapter...	Special features of sites...
◆ *Dinosaur Bob and His Adventures with the Family Lazardo* ◆ *George Shrinks*	◆ *Rolie* Activities ◆ Coloring Pages

About the Author

Children's literature never saw him coming. But one day, when William Joyce arrived, the world of children's books has never been the same. One might say he has the impact of Maurice Sendak. *Newsweek* has acclaimed Mr. Joyce as "one of the top 100 people to watch in the new millennium." The award-winning Mr. Joyce is talented as both a writer and an illustrator and his books have won awards and praise from many sources: the world of movies, the art world, and the literary world. His imaginative writing is filled with wit and humor; his illustrations are masterstrokes of exaggerated scale as seen from the eyes of a child. Born in the fifties in Shreveport, Louisiana, he still resides there with his wife and children. Mr. Joyce leads a very busy life not only writing books, but collaborating with PBS and Disney for television series based on his books, and movie studios producing mega hits like *Toy Story*. Mr. Joyce began drawing at a very young age and always knew he wanted to be an artist. In college, he defied the traditional style that his art teachers tried to get him to emulate and ended up being frustrated that he could not be an artist with his own style. He turned to film making but never lost his love for drawing and illustrating. After college, he published his first children's book. Since 1985, with the publication of *George Shrinks*, Mr. Joyce has had one phenomenal success after another.

Online Author Studies

- "Artist Portfolio: William Joyce," *Storyopolis.com*,
      http://www.storyopolis.com/portfolio-dbp.asp?ArtistID=135 (18 June 2003).
   Twenty-one of Mr. Joyce's illustrations are featured in enlargeable thumbnail sketches and offer details about his medium and artistry.

- Cary, Alice. "The Leaf Men and the Brave Good Bugs: Special Interview with Author and Illustrator, William Joyce," *BookPage.com*,
      http://www.bookpage.com/9610bp/childrens/theleafmen.html (18 June 2003).
   This is an informative interview with the author who details how he gets his ideas and talks about his style.

- Hearn, Michael Patrick. "Exhibits: William Joyce," *National Center for Children's Illustrated Literature*, http://www.nccil.org/exhibit/joyce01.html,
      http://www.nccil.org/collection/txt_permwj.html (18 June 2003).
   These sites give an excellent biographical essay about Mr. Joyce and show the *William Joyce Collection*, a permanent collection at the NCCIL site.

- "Author William Joyce talks about his book, 'George Shrinks'," *Cable News Network*, http://edition.cnn.com/COMMUNITY/transcripts/2000/9/29/joyce/ (18 June 2003).
This transcribed telephone interview with CNN offers insight into the author's work with *George Shrinks* and the PBS television series.

- "Interview with William Joyce," *Readersread.com*, http://www.readersread.com/features/williamjoyce.htm (18 June 2003).
This interview gives details about the life and works of Mr. Joyce, including his work with movies and television.

- Leigh Yawkey Woodson Art Museum. "Gizmos, Gadgets, and Flying Frogs: The Art of William Joyce and David Wiesner," *Traditional Fine Art Online, Inc.* http://www.tfaoi.com/aa/3aa/3aa114.htm (18 June 2003).
This essay is on the works and artistic styles of two famed illustrators.

- "Fluent Reading: Read Together with William Joyce," *PBS Reading Rockets, Launching Young Readers*, http://www.pbs.org/launchingreaders/fluentreading/readtogether.html (18 June 2003).
This essay about the author/illustrator has a four-minute video clip about the world of William Joyce (RealOne Player required), and a link to the popular *George Shrinks* series on PBS's *Bookworm Bunch*.

Lesson Plan Ideas

Dinosaur Bob and His Adventures with the Family Lazardo

> Annotation: While visiting in Africa, the Lazardo family finds a dinosaur and brings him back home with them. The book is a Reading Rainbow selection. [HarperCollins Children's Books, 1999, hardcover ISBN: 0060210753]

- "Reading Rainbow Episode 60: Dinosaur Bob and his Adventures with the Family Lazardo," *GPN Educational Media*, http://gpn.unl.edu/guides/rr/60.pdf (18 June 2003).
Several activities to use with the story are suggested; among them are an alliteration activity, compiling a baseball dictionary, writing a newspaper story, and making a graph of favorite ballpark snacks. The program features the Oakland Athletics.

George Shrinks

> Annotation: George has a series of adventures when he wakes up to find himself the size of a mouse. [HarperCollins Children's Books, 1985, hardcover ISBN: 0060230703]

- "Caregivers: About the Show," *Nelvana Limited/Jade Animation (Shenzhen) Company. A Canada/China Co-production. In association with PBS and produced in association with TVOntario,* http://pbskids.org/georgeshrinks/caregiver/index.html (19 June 2003).

Here, the PBS *George Shrinks* television series is explained and information about the creator, William Joyce, is given. By clicking on "Lesson Plans," teachers can access a comprehensive eighty-page PDF lesson plan, "George Shrinks: See, Think, and Do Activity Guide." The lesson plan has an abundance of integrated lessons to use with the book. Dozens of educational activities, some with reproducible worksheets, are included to extend the themes.

Classroom Center Ideas

Rolie Polie Olie Fun Center

Materials: computer with Internet access, a collection of the Rolie books by William Joyce
Rolie is a robot boy who lives with his family on the Rolie Polie Planet.

- Bookmark the Rolie pages at *Playhouse Disney Online*:
  http://disney.go.com/disneychannel/playhouse/rpo/index.html

- Select from four interactive activities:
  "Pick and Place" (exercises creativity)
  "Online Coloring" (promotes color recognition and creativity)
  "Shapebot Showroom" (promotes shape recognition)
  "Paintball" (promotes color recognition and creativity)

- Select from five interactive games:
  "Star Catcher Olie" (strengthens hand/eye motor skills)
  "Building Blocks" (strengthen comparison and contrasting skills)
  "Connect the Dots" (reinforces number recognition skills)
  "Room Clean" (encourages observation and analysis)
  "Where's Spot?" (strengthens visual discrimination)

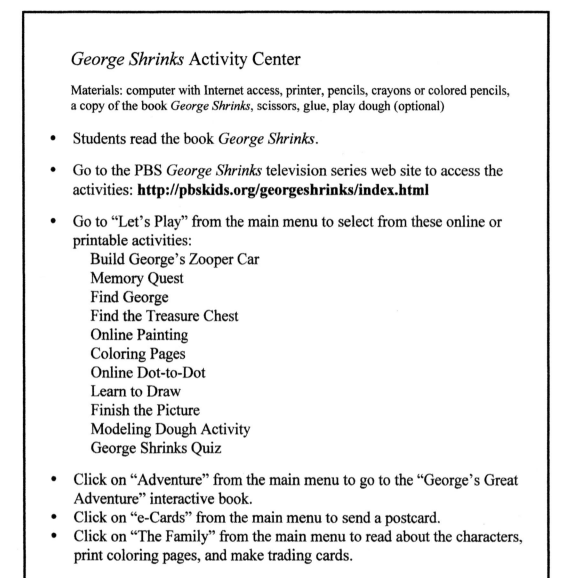

George Shrinks Activity Center

Materials: computer with Internet access, printer, pencils, crayons or colored pencils, a copy of the book *George Shrinks*, scissors, glue, play dough (optional)

- Students read the book *George Shrinks*.

- Go to the PBS *George Shrinks* television series web site to access the activities: **http://pbskids.org/georgeshrinks/index.html**

- Go to "Let's Play" from the main menu to select from these online or printable activities:
  Build George's Zooper Car
  Memory Quest
  Find George
  Find the Treasure Chest
  Online Painting
  Coloring Pages
  Online Dot-to-Dot
  Learn to Draw
  Finish the Picture
  Modeling Dough Activity
  George Shrinks Quiz

- Click on "Adventure" from the main menu to go to the "George's Great Adventure" interactive book.
- Click on "e-Cards" from the main menu to send a postcard.
- Click on "The Family" from the main menu to read about the characters, print coloring pages, and make trading cards.

© Permissions

William Joyce copyrights all art on the web sites.

✉ Making Contact

Write to:
William Joyce
2911 Centenary Blvd.
Shreveport, LA 71104

The Robert Munsch Web Site

RobertMunsch.com

http://www.robertmunsch.com

Description of Site

The Robert Munsch website is a treat for educators and students. It is packed with Munschisms: whimsical stories and poems to tickle anyone's funnybone. A plus for the site is the inclusion of kids' letters, artwork, and stories from all over the world. Mr. Munsch encourages classes to submit writing and drawing samples to the site. There are also photo albums from the hundreds of school visits Mr. Munsch has made. This site is a must-see for writers of all ages. It is motivating to peruse and it is evident that Mr. Munsch loves his work and loves to share and communicate with children and educators.

Best of Site: Virtual Storytelling

The generosity of Mr. Munsch to share his published stories online, in his own voice, makes this feature of his web site a jewel in cyberspace. Dozens of his published stories, many familiar to educators and children, and some not so familiar, are available for listening. There are also unpublished stories included. In order for the stories to be heard, MP3 audio files are required and a download link is available, if needed. Each story must be downloaded prior to listening. It is a captivating experience to hear the stories. And, as with the other pages on his site, the page can be e-mailed to share with others.

Lesson plan ideas in this chapter...	Special features of site...
◆ *Get Out of Bed!*	◆ Illustrated children's stories
◆ *Love You Forever*	◆ Letters and pictures from school visits
◆ *Moira's Birthday*	◆ Printable photos of author for display
◆ *The Paper Bag Princess*	◆ Poetry

About the Author

Mr. Munsch has a six-page autobiography on his website which details his childhood, schooling, jobs, and how he came to be a writer. He relates why he loves working with children and how he got started telling stories while working in day care centers. He liked to write poetry as a child but did not know that he was gifted in storytelling until he met a school librarian who insisted that he start writing down his stories to send to publishers. Mr. Munsch is famous for his school visits. But he doesn't always schedule the visits. Many times, he simply drops in for a surprise visit to a class that has issued him an invitation. Mr. Munsch lives in Canada and travels all around the world to visit schools and tell his stories. He has been named Author of the Year by the Canadian Booksellers Association and is the winner of the Vicky Metcalf Award.

Online Author Studies

- "Amazon.com Talks to Robert Munsch," *Amazon.com*, http://www.amazon.com/exec/obidos/show-interview/m-r-unschobert/102-3534785-6058521 (19 April 2003).
  This site has an interview with Robert Munsch.

- Kasper, Joanne. "Circling with Robert Munsch," http://www.stf.sk.ca/teaching_res/library/teach_mat_centre/tmc/P11233/P11233.htm (19 April 2003).
  This site offers biographical information and discusses many of Robert Munsch's favorite stories for literature circles.

- Khan, Iram and James Horner. "Q and A with Robert Munsch," *Canadian Content*, http://www.canadiancontent.ca/issues/0499munsch.html (19 April 2003).
  This site has an interview with the author.

- "Robert Munsch," *Annick Press*, http://www.annickpress.com/ai/munsch.html (19 April 2003).
  This site has a biography of the author and a list of his works.

- "Robert Munsch," *Scholastic, Inc.* http://www2.scholastic.com/teachers/authorsandbooks/authorstudies/authorhome.jhtml?authorID=66&collateralID=5247 (20 April 2003).
  This site has a biography, an interview, a booklist, and a link to the author's site.

- "Robert Munsch Featured on CBC's Life and Times," *Firefly Books Press Release*, http://www.fireflybooks.com/Kids/Munschbio.html (19 April 2003).
  This site has a brief biography and a description of *Love You Forever* with sample illustrations and text from the book.

Lesson Plan Ideas

Get Out of Bed!

> Annotation: Amy stays up late watching TV and will not get up to go to school the next morning. Finally, her parents pick up her bed, with Amy still in it, and carry it to school. [Scholastic, 2002, paperback ISBN: 0439388511]

- Holmen, Ina and Marg Mayotte. "Making Connections with Reader's Theatre," http://www.stf.sk.ca/src/teach_mat_centre/tmc/P11235/Reader's%20Theatre.pdf (20 April 2003).
  Scroll down to page 15 to view a reader's theatre script for this story. Adobe Acrobat is required to view this PDF file. There is also a blank script map located on page 13. The entire site is a good overview of reader's theatre.

Love You Forever

> Annotation: One of the most published books in children's literature, this is the lyrical story of a mother's feelings toward her son. [Firefly Books, LTD, 1988, paperback ISBN: 0920668372]

- Bray, Latresa J. "Teacher View: Love You Forever," *Townview Elementary School, Dayton, OH,* http://www.eduplace.com/tview/tviews/l/loveyouforever.html (20 April 2003).
  Three activities to use with the book are outlined: Family and Friends Feast, Letters of Love, and Love Poem.

Moira's Birthday

> Annotation: Moira matter-of-factly solves the many disasters befalling her family, unlike her parents who have trouble coping. [Firefly Books LTD, 1988, paperback ISBN: 0920303838]

- Kohner, Stephen. "Reader's Theatre: Moira's Birthday," *Baie Comeau High School,* http://www.qesn.meq.gouv.qc.ca/schools/bchs/rtheatre/sample.htm (20 April 2003).
  This script is the basis for an enjoyable and educational language arts activity.

The Paper Bag Princess

> Annotation: Princess Elizabeth is to marry Prince Ronald when a dragon attacks the castle and kidnaps Ronald. Elizabeth, wearing only a paper bag, finds the dragon, outwits him, and rescues Ronald. When Ronald sees Elizabeth's disheveled appearance, he thinks twice about wanting to marry her. Elizabeth decides she is much better off without this prince. [Firefly Books, LTD, 1985, paperback ISBN 0920236162]

- "Elements of a Fairy Tale," *Putnam Valley Elementary School, NY*,
  http://putnamvalleyschools.org/ft/02Elements.html (20 April 2003).
  This is a good lesson to explain the characteristics of fairy tales. After reading a traditional fairy tale, compare and contrast with Robert Munsch's version.

- "Fairy Tale Mural," *Putnam Valley Elementary School, NY*,
  http://putnamvalleyschools.org/ft/04Mural.html (20 April 2003).
  This idea is a good way to extend *The Paper Bag Princess*, or any fairy tale.

- "Paper Bag Princess," *Kaleidoscope Family Child Care*,
  http://kaleidoscopecare.tripod.com/rmunsch.html (20 April 2003).
  This site has wonderful illustrations to accompany the story. Use to decorate the classroom or for a class play.

- Payne, Jullie. "TeacherView: The Paper Bag Princess," *Maeser Elementary School, Provo, UT*, http://www.eduplace.com/tview/tviews/p/paperbagprincess.html
  (20 April 2003).
  This language arts activity uses paper bags for students to write their own fairy tales after hearing the story. Students decorate their bags to help tell the story.

- Mrs. Zakowsky. "The Paper Bag Princess," *Central Falls School District, RI*,
  http://www.ri.net/schools/Central_Falls/ch/heazak/dragon/dragon.html
  (19 April 2003).
  This integrated lesson plan has good ideas for extending the story.

© Permissions

No restrictions could be found on the web site. Adhere to Federal copyright laws.

⊠ Making Contact

Robert Munsch
15 Sharon Place
Guelph, Ontario, Canada
N1H 7V2

Classroom Center Ideas

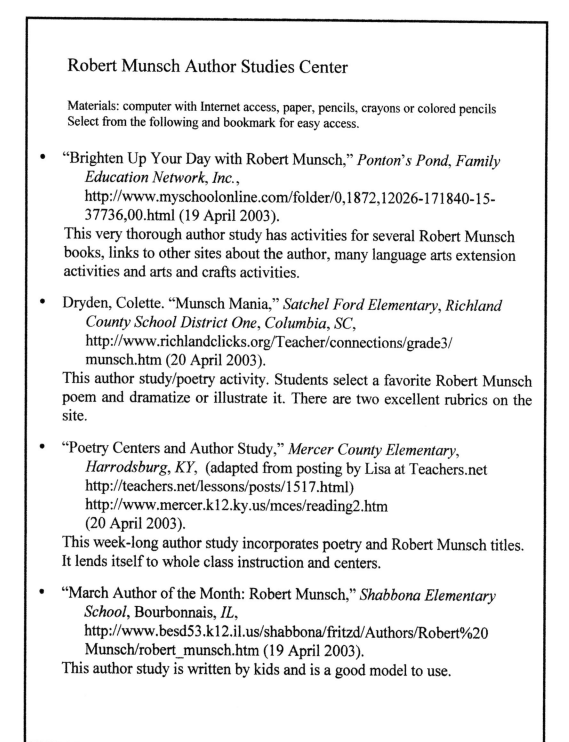

Robert Munsch Author Studies Center

Materials: computer with Internet access, paper, pencils, crayons or colored pencils
Select from the following and bookmark for easy access.

- "Brighten Up Your Day with Robert Munsch," *Ponton's Pond, Family Education Network, Inc.*,
  http://www.myschoolonline.com/folder/0,1872,12026-171840-15-37736,00.html (19 April 2003).
  This very thorough author study has activities for several Robert Munsch books, links to other sites about the author, many language arts extension activities and arts and crafts activities.

- Dryden, Colette. "Munsch Mania," *Satchel Ford Elementary, Richland County School District One, Columbia, SC*,
  http://www.richlandclicks.org/Teacher/connections/grade3/munsch.htm (20 April 2003).
  This author study/poetry activity. Students select a favorite Robert Munsch poem and dramatize or illustrate it. There are two excellent rubrics on the site.

- "Poetry Centers and Author Study," *Mercer County Elementary, Harrodsburg, KY*, (adapted from posting by Lisa at Teachers.net http://teachers.net/lessons/posts/1517.html)
  http://www.mercer.k12.ky.us/mces/reading2.htm
  (20 April 2003).
  This week-long author study incorporates poetry and Robert Munsch titles. It lends itself to whole class instruction and centers.

- "March Author of the Month: Robert Munsch," *Shabbona Elementary School*, Bourbonnais, *IL*,
  http://www.besd53.k12.il.us/shabbona/fritzd/Authors/Robert%20Munsch/robert_munsch.htm (19 April 2003).
  This author study is written by kids and is a good model to use.

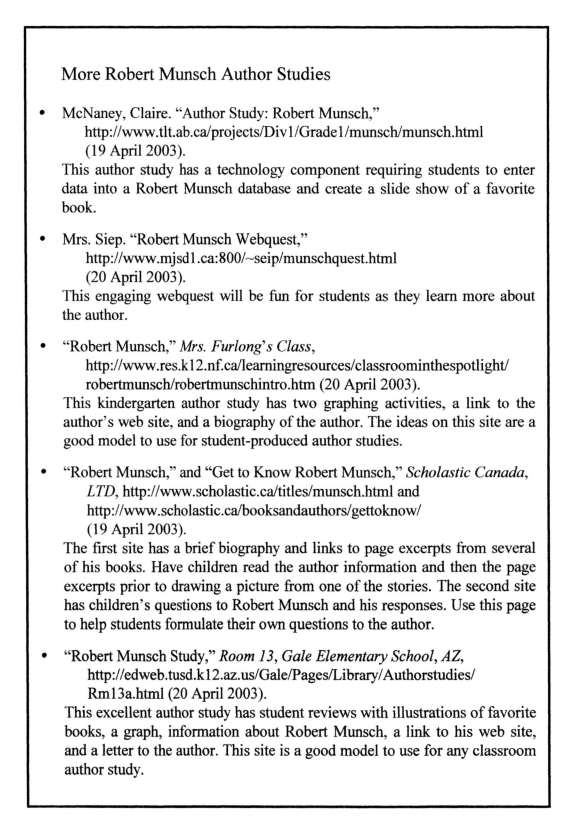

More Robert Munsch Author Studies

- McNaney, Claire. "Author Study: Robert Munsch,"
    http://www.tlt.ab.ca/projects/Div1/Grade1/munsch/munsch.html
    (19 April 2003).
  This author study has a technology component requiring students to enter data into a Robert Munsch database and create a slide show of a favorite book.

- Mrs. Siep. "Robert Munsch Webquest,"
    http://www.mjsd1.ca:800/~seip/munschquest.html
    (20 April 2003).
  This engaging webquest will be fun for students as they learn more about the author.

- "Robert Munsch," *Mrs. Furlong's Class*,
    http://www.res.k12.nf.ca/learningresources/classroominthespotlight/
    robertmunsch/robertmunschintro.htm (20 April 2003).
  This kindergarten author study has two graphing activities, a link to the author's web site, and a biography of the author. The ideas on this site are a good model to use for student-produced author studies.

- "Robert Munsch," and "Get to Know Robert Munsch," *Scholastic Canada,
    LTD*, http://www.scholastic.ca/titles/munsch.html and
    http://www.scholastic.ca/booksandauthors/gettoknow/
    (19 April 2003).
  The first site has a brief biography and links to page excerpts from several of his books. Have children read the author information and then the page excerpts prior to drawing a picture from one of the stories. The second site has children's questions to Robert Munsch and his responses. Use this page to help students formulate their own questions to the author.

- "Robert Munsch Study," *Room 13, Gale Elementary School, AZ*,
    http://edweb.tusd.k12.az.us/Gale/Pages/Library/Authorstudies/
    Rm13a.html (20 April 2003).
  This excellent author study has student reviews with illustrations of favorite books, a graph, information about Robert Munsch, a link to his web site, and a letter to the author. This site is a good model to use for any classroom author study.

The Laura Joffe Numeroff Web Site

Laura Numeroff's (very own) Web Site

http://www.lauranumeroff.com

Description of Site

The author's web site provides excellent autobiographical information and photographs of the author. The biographical information is divided into three stages: the childhood years, college years, and adult years. It is appealing in appearance and has pages for teachers, parents, and students. The site contains reviews of her books, a section on the books featured on the Oprah show, and activities for students. Students will love to see the well-known titles depicted in other languages and the picture of a Tokyo city bus decorated with her mouse character. Click on the music icon to hear music at the site.

Best of Site: Story Starters

This idea from the author is one she uses when she visits schools and can be found in the "Teachers Section." Give students story starters based on the pattern in the popular Laura Numeroff circle stories. Or, let students make up their own story starters. For example, "If you give a [puppy] a ..." Have students finish the sentence. Then have the whole class participate in finishing the entire story. Go to the "Kids Fun" section of the web site for other ideas to inspire creative writing activities. Another good feature of the site to use with the "Story Starters" activities is the link to *DLTK's* "If You Give a Mouse a Cookie" pages. These are crafts, coloring pages, and language arts activities to use in conjunction with the book. To access, go to:
http://www.dltk-kids.com/books/mousecookie.html.

Lesson plan ideas in this chapter...	Special features of site...
◆ *If You Give a Mouse a Cookie*	◆ Find the Pig Game
◆ *If You Give a Moose a Muffin*	◆ E-postcards
◆ *If You Give a Pig a Pancake*	◆ Coloring pages

About the Author

Laura Joffe Numeroff is best known for her revolutionary circular stories that started with the overwhelming success of *If You Give a Mouse a Cookie*, illustrated by Felicia Bond. Ms. Numeroff is the recipient of numerous awards for her books. She attended Pratt Institute, where she intended to study fashion design like her sister, but soon left when she realized that was not the career for her. She then enrolled in Parsons College and received a degree in fine arts in 1975. She had her first book contract right out of college and has been writing and entertaining children ever since.

Online Author Studies

- "Behind The Books: A Visit with Children's Book Team Laura Numeroff and Felicia Bond," *Ingram Book Company*, http://www.ingrambookgroup.com/Company_info/ibchtml/Resource_Center/ Whats_New/bb_numeroff_bond.asp (26 April 2003).
  This site has an interview with the author discussing how she got her ideas for *If You Give a Pig a Pancake*. It ends with a recipe for Pig's favorite pancakes.

- "Interview: If You Take a Mouse to School," *HarperCollins.com*, http://www.harperchildrens.com/catalog/book_interview_xml.asp?isbn=00602832 89 (26 April 2003).
  This publisher's site has a lengthy interview with the author and a link to the biography of Felicia Bond, the illustrator of many of the author's books. By clicking on "More books by this author," one can read about all of her books and see excerpts.

- "Laura Numeroff," *Kidsreads.com*, http://www.kidsreads.com/authors/au-numeroff-laura.asp (26 April 2003).
  This site has the author's autobiography and an interview with the author.

- "Laura Numeroff Biography," *Scholastic.com*, http://www2.scholastic.com/teachers/authorsandbooks/authorstudies/authorhome. jhtml?authorID=69&collateralID=5253 (26 April 2003).
  This site has an autobiography and a booklist, with reviews, of the author's books.

- Richards, Linda. "January Interview: Laura Numeroff," *January Magazine*, http://www.januarymagazine.com/profiles/primages/numeroff.html (26 April 2003).
  This site has an in-depth interview with the author and includes information about circular stories.

Lesson Plan Ideas

If You Give a Mouse a Cookie

> Annotation: Children will delight in this circular story. A cookie is simply not enough for this mouse. [HarperCollins Children's Books, 1985, hardcover ISBN: 0060245867]

- Hubbard, Michelle. "If You Give a Mouse a Cookie," *Hubbard's Cupboard*, http://www.hubbardscupboard.org/if_you_give_a_mouse_a_cookie.html (26 April 2003).
  Fifteen math and literacy activities are showcased on this site. The activities can be used to extend the story while integrating math skills.

- Koch, Amy. "Repetition and Prediction," *A to Z Teacher Stuff*, http://www.atozteacherstuff.com/lessons/RepititionandPrediction.shtml (26 April 2003).
  Use this kindergarten lesson idea with any of the author's circular stories. Students will create a class story entitled, *If You Give a Kindergartener ....*

- Mrs. Farrar. "If You Give a Mouse a Cookie Webquest," *WNEO.org*, http://wneo.org/WebQuests/TeacherWebQuests/mouse/mouse.htm (26 April 2003).
  Paired students will complete several activities to complete the webquest task.

- Smith, Katy J. "TeacherViews: If You Give a Mouse a Cookie," *Education Place, Houghton Mifflin Company*, http://www.eduplace.com/tview/pages/i/If_You_Give_a_Mouse_a_Cookie_Laura_Joffe_Numeroff.html (26 April 2003).
  This lesson is about writing a class circular story using the concepts of cause and effect. A suggested title is *If You Give a First Grader a* [noun].

- Suiter, Mary. "If You Give a Mouse a Cookie," *Economics and Children's Literature, Supplement 2, SPEC Publishers Inc.* and *Economic Education*, http://ecedweb.unomaha.edu/lessons/mouse.htm (26 April 2003).
  This lesson has many good extension activities for teaching cause and effect, sequencing, recall, and making predictions.

- Weeg, Patricia A. "If You Give a Mouse a Cookie," *GlobalClassroom.org*, http://www.globalclassroom.org/mouse.html (26 April 2003).
  This classroom site has student letters about the book, with photographs.

- Weiler, Danielle. "Sample Spanish Lesson Plan: Si le das una galletita a un ratón," Illinois State University, http://www.coe.ilstu.edu/portfolios/students/feo/feos2001/dbweile/Spanishlesson.htm (26 April 2003).
This lesson includes bilingual vocabulary words and discussion questions in Spanish.

If You Give a Moose a Muffin

> Annotation: Another delightful circular story will that captivate children. [HarperCollins Children's Books, 1991, hardcover ISBN: 0060244062]

- Payne, Julie. "TeacherViews: If You Give a Moose a Muffin," *Education Place, Houghton Mifflin Company,* http://www.eduplace.com/tview/pages/i/If_You_Give_a_Moose_a_Muffin_Laura_Joffe_Numeroff.html (26 April 2003). [Scroll midway down page.]
This is an activity on using transitional words in writing. Making circle books is also described.

- Weber, Heidi. "TeacherViews: If You Give a Moose a Muffin," *Education Place, Houghton Mifflin Company,* http://www.eduplace.com/tview/pages/i/If_You_Give_a_Moose_a_Muffin_Laura_Joffe_Numeroff.html (26 April 2003).
This is a sequencing activity to use with the book.

If You Give a Pig a Pancake

> Annotation: A mouse, then a moose, now a pig. Children and teachers love these circular stories. [HarperCollins Children's Books, 1998, library binding ISBN: 0060266872]

- Koch, Amy. "If You Give a Pig a Pancake: P is for Pancake," *A to Z Teacher Stuff,* http://atozteacherstuff.com/lessons/Pancakes.shtml (30 June 2003).
This is a cooking activity to use with the book while learning about the letter "P".

- Phagan, Staci. "If You Give a Pig a Pancake, What Happens?" *S. L. Mason Elementary School, Valdosta State University,* http://www.valdosta.edu/~slphagan/paint.html (30 June 2003).
This lesson plan uses a software painting program to draw pictures from the story. Click on the Lesson Plan link for details. View examples of students' work.

Classroom Center Ideas

Mouse Fun Center

Materials: computer with Internet access, printer, crayons or colored pencils, the books *If You Take a Mouse to School*, *If You Take a Mouse to the Movies*, and *If You Give a Mouse a Cookie*

- Download the screensaver for this character to a classroom computer:
  http://www.harperchildrens.com/hch/mouse/images/fun.asp

- Take the online quiz after reading the book, *If You Give a Mouse a Cookie*:
  http://familyeducation.com/quiz/0,1399,2-15343,00.html

- Select a picture from the book to color:
  http://familyeducation.com/printables/package/0,2358,22-15950,00.html

- Build and send a mouse e-card:
  http://www.harperchildrens.com/hch/mouse/mouse.asp

- Select from several interactive activities and printable games and puzzles:
  http://www.harperchildrens.com/hch/mouse/mouse_activities.asp or
  http://www.harperchildrens.com/hch/picture/series/mouse/

- Complete and illustrate the *If You Give a Mouse a Cookie* worksheet:
  http://www.sanjuan.edu/select/3t/lyda/Worksheet.gif

- Print and complete a copy of the math story problems for this story:
  http://www.hubbardscupboard.org/if_you_give_a_mouse_a_cookie.html

Laura Numeroff Author Study Center

Materials: computer with Internet access, printer, a collection of Laura Numeroff circular books, paper to create a storyboard, software for word processing, a paint program, and/or a multimedia slide show program such as Mpower, KidPix, or PowerPoint, binder

- Select one or more of the web sites listed in the section "Online Author Studies." Read the biographical information and interviews.

- Complete the author study worksheet.

- Read books written by Laura Numeroff.

- In cooperative groups, create a class book or a multimedia slide show patterned after the author's circular stories. Use Carol Hornik's Teachnet Project Internet lesson for guidelines:
  http://teachersnetwork.org/teachnetnyc/chornik/authorstudy.htm

- Present and share students' creations when finished.

- Visit the author's web site and look at letters she has received from children:
  http://www.lauranumeroff.com/mail_bag.htm
  Then write a letter of your own to the author and send it, after your teacher has seen it, by clicking on the e-mail link from the home page.

© Permissions

The images and text found on the web site are either owned by Laura Numeroff, or by one of the publishers that she and the many illustrators are represented by. Re-use of this material is prohibited without the expressed written consent of the owner.

✉ Making Contact

E-mail:
mail@lauranumeroff.com

Beatrix Potter's Peter Rabbit

World of Peter Rabbit

http://www.peterrabbit.com

Description of Site

This exquisite site from the publisher, Frederick Warne, is filled with illustrations from the famous watercolors for which Beatrix Potter is known. The site also contains black and white photographs of the author in the English countryside. It is filled with detailed information about the author's life and the legacy she left to the world. It has many interactive activities for children in "Tom Kitten's Playground," such as coloring pages, word searches, games, and puzzles. There is a "Squirrel Nutkin Film Show" in honor of the 100th anniversary of *The Tale of Squirrel Nutkin,* first published in 1903, with video clips from several of the Potter stories. One will find over a dozen e-cards from the "Jemima Puddleduck E-cards" pages. The are many pages from the author's many sketchbooks, schoolbooks, and letters. Click on "Events and Press Office," then "Links and Awards" for dozens of other sites about the author, her work, and her residences. There are many web sites about Beatrix Potter, but this one is sure to be a hit with teachers and students.

Best of Site: Meet the Characters

Click on "Fun" from the home page, then "Meet the Characters" to access this excellent component of the site. There are two features in this section: "Make Friends" and "Storytime." From the "Make Friends" pages, one will find monthly character sketches and detailed histories about selected titles. From the "Storytime" pages, one can listen to the wonderful stories from Beatrix Potter as they are read aloud and also follow along by reading the text and viewing the illustrations.

Lesson plan ideas in this chapter...	Special features of site...
• *The Tale of Peter Rabbit* • *The Tale of Benjamin Bunny* • *The Tale of the Flopsy Bunnies*	• E-Postcards • Games, Coloring Pages, Puzzles • Video Clips

About the Author

Beatrix Potter is one of the most beloved storytellers and illustrators of children's stories, which are considered treasures in the world of children's literature. Her works have become some of the most famous ever written for children. Her gift to us transcends literary and artistic works; she was also a naturalist and was deeply devoted to the preservation of farms and the countryside of the Lake District in England. At her death, she bequeathed 4000 acres to The National Trust, an organization dedicated to carrying out the preservation of the land she loved.

Beatrix Potter started at a very young age to draw and paint with watercolors. She kept journals, sketchbooks, and schoolbooks using as subjects her menagerie of pets and animals discovered on holidays and outings. Raised in a strict Victorian household, she and her brother Bertram were sheltered and mostly reared by governesses and nursery servants. *The Tale of Peter Rabbit*, her first published book, was originally rejected by six publishers. Not until she printed the book herself did Frederick Warne and Co. finally publish it in 1903. Beatrix Potter originally wrote the story to an ex-governess's sick child in the form of a picture letter in 1893. The character, Peter, was based on her own pet, Peter Piper, a Belgian buck rabbit. Nearly all the characters in her twenty-three stories were based on her own pets. Her home in the Lake District, Hill Top Farm, was the setting for many of her stories. Beatrix Potter was also well-known for her lovely watercolor landscapes and botanical drawings. Today, visitors can visit the places where she lived, see the countryside that she loved, and visit the museums that house her original works and memorabilia.

See also *The Beatrix Potter Society* web site for more information about the life, works, homes, area attractions, and events pertaining to Beatrix Potter:
http://www.beatrixpottersociety.org.uk/

Online Author Studies

- "Beatrix Potter," *Frederick Warne & Co. Limited,*
  http://www.peterrabbit.com/beatrixpotter/beatrixpotter3.cfm (17 May 2003).
  This section from the *World of Peter Rabbit* web site provides detailed information
  about the author's life, her artistry, and her devotion to Lake District preservation.

- "Beatrix Potter," *VisitCumbria.com,* http://www.visitcumbria.com/bpotter.htm
  (17 May 2003).
  This site is filled with links to Lake District farms, homes, vacation spots, libraries,
  landscapes, museums, and people pertinent to Beatrix Potter.

- "Beatrix Potter: More Than a Rabbit's Tale," *Twingroves District 96,*
  http://www.twingroves.district96.k12.il.us/Easter/BPotter.html (31 May 2003).
  This article tells about Miss Potter's life and works.

- Bittner, Terrie. "Past Times: Beatrix Potter: More than Peter Rabbit's Mother,"
  Suite101.com, http://www.suite101.com/mypage.cfm/womens_history/235
  (10 May 2003).
  This web site has a wealth of interesting details about Beatrix Potter's childhood and
  how her career began as a writer and illustrator.

- Clark, Ann McAllister. "Information on Authors: Beatrix Potter," *TomFolio.com,*
  http://tomfolio.com/AuthorInfo/BeatrixPotter.asp (31 May 2003).
  This article tells how Miss Potter became affiliated with publisher Frederick Warne
  and Company, Warne family members, and their impact on her books.

- "Google Images for Beatrix Potter," *Google.com,*
  http://images.google.com/images?q=Beatrix+Potter (11 May 2003).
  This is a good site to view photographs of the author, illustrations from her books,
  her homes, and her letters.

- Liukkonen, Petri. "(Helen) Beatrix Potter (1866-1943)," *Books and Writers,*
  http://www.kirjasto.sci.fi/bpotter.htm (10 May 2003).
  This site has a biography and a bibliography of the author's works.

- Ortakales, Denise. "Helen Beatrix Potter," *Women Children's Book Illustrators,*
  http://www.ortakales.com/illustrators/Potter.html (11 May 2003).
  This is an excellent site for detailed information about the author's childhood,
  education, career, the influences that helped shape her style, excerpts from her journals,
  and pages from her sketchbook.

- Straw, Deborah. "More Than Just Bunnies: The Legacy of Beatrix Potter," *Literary Traveler, The Nomad Group,* http://www.literarytraveler.com/europe/potter.htm (31 May 2003). This site has an excellent, very detailed biography about the author.

- Tonnessen, M. "An Author Study of Beatrix Potter," *Dickerson School, Chester, NJ,* http://home.att.net/~cattonn/potter.html (10 May 2003). This author study also has activities for art, music, language arts, and science.

Lesson Plan Ideas

The Tale of Peter Rabbit

The Tale of Peter Rabbit Annotation: The story of Peter who disobeys his mother by going into Mr. McGregor's garden and almost gets caught. [Frederick Warne and Co., 2002, hardcover ISBN: 0723247706]

The Ultimate Peter Rabbit Annotation: This book presents the life and work of Beatrix Potter through drawings, photographs, letters, journal entries, and excerpts. [Dorling Kindersley, 2002, hardcover ISBN: 0789485389]

- "Beatrix Potter's Naughty Animal Tales," *EDSITEment, National Endowment for the Humanities,* http://edsitement.neh.gov/view_lesson_plan.asp?id=386 (10 May 2003). This lesson plan, although intended for intermediate grades, has excellent discussion questions, writing activities, and a link to a Story Chart to print for students to record the literary elements in the stories. It also has links to other sites about Beatrix Potter, the Victorian era, and online stories by Beatrix Potter. Use aspects of this site as a guideline to adapt lessons for the primary grades.

- Christiansen, Judy. "How Well Do You Know Peter Rabbit?" *Quia Quiz,* http://www.quia.com/tq/109403.html (10 May 2003). Students can take this online quiz after reading the story.

- Corrado, Maria. "Webquest: Peter Rabbit and the Tortoise and the Hare," *John F. Kennedy School, Quebec City, CA,*
  http://olp.swlauriersb.qc.ca/webquest/peterrabbit/petertortoisehare.htm
  (10 Mary 2003).

This lesson plan, although for two stories, may be used with just the Peter Rabbit story. It contains four worksheets that may be printed for students to answer after reading the story.

- TeacherHelp. "The Tale of Peter Rabbit," *Wright Group Publishing,*
  http://www.teacherhelp.com/your_classroom/lesson_plans/lessonpln11.html
  (10 May 2003).

This integrated lesson plan contains good language arts activities to extend the story, such as practice with compound words, sequencing, homophones, and literary elements. It also has activities for the study of fruits, vegetables, and gardening.

The Tale of Benjamin Bunny

> Annotation: Peter's mischievous cousin, Benjamin Bunny, persuades him to go back to Mr. McGregor's garden to retrieve his abandoned clothes. [Frederick Warne and Co., 2002, hardcover ISBN: 0723247730]

- "E-Readers Lesson Plan: The Tale of Benjamin Bunny," *E-Readers, Seminole County Public Schools, FL,*
  http://www.ereaders.scps.k12.fl.us/lessons/benbunnylesson.htm
  (11 May 2003).

This lesson plan successfully integrates technology with language arts. It utilizes *Inspiration* software to analyze the story parts.

- Take an online comprehension quiz after reading *The Tale of Benjamin Bunny:*
  http://comsewogue.k12.ny.us/~ssilverman/bunnies/benjamin/
  benjaminc.htm (11 May 2003).

This quiz provides feedback to students and gives a score when finished.

The Tale of the Flopsy Bunnies

Annotation: The six Flopsy Bunnies narrowly escape the dangers in Mr. McGregor's garden. [Penguin USA, 1969, hardcover ISBN: 0723234698]

- Silverman, S. "Gap Fill Exercise: The Flopsy Bunnies," *Comsewogue School, NY*, http://comsewogue.k12.ny.us/~ssilverman/bunnies/flopsybun/flopsybunc.htm (11 May 2003).

This online reading comprehension quiz, in fill-in-the-blank format, provides hints and allows students to check their answers.

Classroom Center Ideas

Poetry Center

Materials: computer with Internet access, drawing paper, pencils, crayons or colored pencils

- Go to *The Horn Book Virtual History Exhibit* to view "Verse Illustrated by Beatrix Potter": **http://www.hbook.com/exhibit/art_potter1.html**

- Have students read the poem by Beatrix Potter and look at the illustrations.

- Students will write and illustrate their own animal poems using the Beatrix Potter poem as a template for their poems.

- When all students have completed their poems, bind them into a class book or display them on a bulletin board.

E-Reading Center*

Materials: computer with Internet access, headphones , dictionary, paper, pencils

There are many e-book sites with full texts of the Beatrix Potter stories. These listed below have been selected for their visual appeal and larger fonts for younger children.

- Go to *Wired for Books Kids' Corner* to view full text with illustrations for many of Beatrix Potter's tales:
  http://home.att.net/~cattonn/potter.html
  This site is appealing with its slide show format.

- Go to The University of Virginia's *Electronic Text Center: Young Readers Collection*:
  http://etext.lib.virginia.edu/subjects/Young-Readers.html
  Scroll down to the "P's" for the links to fifteen Beatrix Potter titles. These e-stories are made even more valuable because they show facsimiles of Beatrix Potter's original sketchbooks, illustrations, and text. The thumbnails can be enlarged for better viewing.

- Go to *Acacia Vignettes* to read five Beatrix Potter stories:
  http://acacia.pair.com/Acacia.Vignettes/Stories.html
  Scroll midway down the page to see the links to these stories.

- Read from seven Beatrix Potter stories online at *Bedtime Stories from Briana's Playroom*:
  http://members.tripod.com/ah_coo/bedtime_stories.htm
  Scroll midway down the page to see the links to the stories.

- Read from three Beatrix Potter selections at *The Rabbit Reading Room*:
  http://members.iinet.net.au/~rabbit/rabroom.htm
  This unique site has full text and hot links to an online dictionary for words students may not know.

- View three Beatrix Potter stories at *Marsha's Rabbit Tales* site:
  http://www.geocities.com/Athens/Forum/5452/tales.html
  These stories were taken from the e-texts at *Project Gutenberg* with font changes for easier reading, one page at a time.

* Care should be taken to observe copyright restrictions when downloading or printing from these sites. Refer to each site's *Conditions of Use* pages for details.

Peter Rabbit Activity Center

Materials: computer with Internet access, printer, pencils

- Go to Enchanted Learning's *Rabbits* page and read about rabbits:
  **http://www.enchantedlearning.com/subjects/mammals/farm/
  Rabbitprintout.shtml**

- After reading, take the *Rabbit Quiz* at Enchanted Learning:
  **http://www.enchantedlearning.com/subjects/mammals/farm/Rabbit
  quiz.shtml**

- Go to the online paint page at Enchanted Learning and paint a rabbit:
  **http://www.enchantedlearning.com/paint/subjects/mammals/farm/
  Rabbitprintout.shtml**

Mr. McGregor's Garden Center

Materials: computer with Internet access, printer, drawing paper, crayons, pencils

- Go to Enchanted Learning's *Label the Vegetables* page:
  http://www.enchantedlearning.com/food/label/veg/
  Print a copy of the worksheet, then label the vegetables and color.

- For fun, label the vegetables in other languages, such as Spanish, German, French, Italian, or Russian. Go to Enchanted Learning's Home Page at **http://www.enchantedlearning.com/Home.html** and scroll down to *Languages*. An answer key is provided.

- Go to children's garden drawings from *Havencroft Elementary School*, Olathe, Kansas:
  http://aggie-horticulture.tamu.edu/kinder/art/gallery1.html
  View the pictures, then have students create their own garden drawings.

- Play S. Seagraves' "Garden Concentration online":
  **http://www.geocities.com/Athens/Atrium/5924/concentrateapplet/
  concentration.htm**

© Permissions

⊠ Making Contact

E-mail:
peterrabbit@penguin.co.uk
or,
info@beatrixpottersociety.org.uk

Write to:
Marketing Director or Online Manager
Frederick Warne and Co., LTD
80 Strand
London WC2R ORL

H. A. and Margret Rey's Curious George

Houghton Mifflin's Books for Children's Curious George

http://www.curiousgeorge.com

Description of Site

This dazzling web site from Houghton Mifflin opens with the signature lemon yellow background and immediately dazzles the eye. The home page depicts the impish monkey having a birthday party with his friends to celebrate the sixty-plus years since the publication of the first Curious George book in 1941. Links surround the main image and include the history of Curious George, a biography of the creators, H. A. and Margret Rey, a link to original art and memorabilia from the de Grummond Children's Literature Collection at the University of Southern Mississippi, and puzzles, games, and downloads. The site has it all for fans of Curious George. Of particular value to educators is the inclusion of numerous educational activities to enhance the curriculum.

Best of Site: The Curious George Birthday Party Kit and Teacher's Guide

This part of the web site will amaze teachers and delight students. From the home page, click on *Media Center* to access these PDF files (Adobe Acrobat required). A twenty-page birthday party kit, created when *Curious George* was celebrating his 60th birthday, and a seventeen-page teacher's guide can be found. Teachers can print these booklets for a wealth of curriculum-related activities to use with the Curious George books. The guides have games, puzzles, language arts activities, math activities, and much more.

Lesson plan ideas in this chapter...	Special features of site...
◆ *Curious George Rides a Bike*	◆ Dozens of reproducibles
◆ *Curious George Gets a Medal*	◆ Virtual Literary Exhibit
◆ *Curious George Learns the Alphabet*	◆ Games, coloring sheets, puzzles
◆ *Curious George Takes a Job*	◆ Biographical information

About the Authors

H. A. (Hans) and Margret Rey had a fascinating life. They were both born in Hamburg, Germany in 1898 and 1906, respectively. Hans lived near the world-famous Hagenbeck Zoo and developed a lifelong love of animals and drawing. They briefly met in Hamburg during their childhood years but Margret left the city to study art. They were reunited in 1935, in Rio de Janeiro, where Hans was working in his family's business selling bathtubs. Both had moved to Brazil to escape the political climate in Europe. Margret convinced Hans to leave the family business and they soon were married. While on their European honeymoon, they fell in love with Paris and decided to make it their home. Hans produced cartoons for newspapers and was discovered by a French publisher who urged him to write a children's book. This is how they came to collaborate on their first book, *Raffy and the Nine Monkeys* (*Cecily G. and the Nine Monkeys*, in English). Curious George was one of the nine monkeys and this is where he made his debut. Soon after, they began to write a book just for Curious George. The Reys, however, both Jewish, found their lives in danger when the Nazis were about to invade Paris. On June 14, 1940, they fled Paris on homemade bicycles, with very little, but they did manage to take the unfinished Curious George manuscript with them. They barely escaped because the Nazis invaded later that same day. They made their way across the French border into Spain, then on to Lisbon, then Brazil, and finally, New York. Little did they know that their mischievous monkey character would revolutionize children's literature worldwide.

Online Author Studies

- "About H. A. and Margret Rey," *Curious George, Houghton Mifflin Company*, http://www.houghtonmifflinbooks.com/features/cgsite/abouthaandmargret rey.shtml (17 June 2003).
  This informative biography is from the *Curious George* web site.

- de Grummond Collection. "Curious George Goes to Hattiesburg: The Life and Work of H. A. and Margret Rey," *University of Southern Mississippi*, http://www.lib.usm.edu/%7Edegrum/html/collectionhl/Curious%20George/ opener.shtml (17 June 2003).
  This is a must-see site to learn about the Reys, their contributions to children's literature, and their bequest to the de Grummond Collection.

- de Grummond Collection. "H. A. and Margret Rey Collection," *University of Southern Mississippi*, http://www.lib.usm.edu/~degrum/html/collectionhl/ ch-reys.shtml (30 June 2003).
  This is an introduction to the collection and background on how it got started.

- Department of English. "Margret Rey," *Kansas State University*, http://www-personal.ksu.edu/~akp9999/main.html (17 June 2003).
  This site has several sections about the author including a biography, a bibliography, essays on her writing and artistic styles, the background behind the stories, and the prevalent themes in the stories.

- "The History of Curious George and the Reys," *Curious George, Houghton Mifflin Company*, http://www.houghtonmifflinbooks.com/features/cgsite/curiousaboutgeorge.shtml (17 June 2003).
  This is a fascinating history and interview with the Reys.

- "Meet the Writers: H. A. and Margret Rey," *Barnesandnoble.com*, http://www.barnesandnoble.com/writers/writerdetails.asp?cid=968100 (17 June 2003).
  This biography about the Reys tells why Margret's name did not appear on some of the earliest covers.

Lesson Plan Ideas

Curious George Rides a Bike

> Annotation: Curious George is at it again when he gets a new bicycle and delivers newspapers, gets sidetracked making paper boats, ends up performing at a circus, and ends up a hero when he rescues a baby bear. [Houghton Mifflin Company, 1976, hardcover ISBN: 039516964X]

- "Curious George Rides a Bike," *Curious George, Houghton Mifflin Company,* http://www.houghtonmifflinbooks.com/features/cgsite/cgtgpdfs/cgtgnespaperart. pdf (17 June 2003).
These two PDF files offer two printable writing activities to use after reading the story. They can be useful in teaching how to write newspaper articles.

Curious George Gets a Medal

> Annotation: Curious George cannot seem to do anything right. He floods the house, lets out all the pigs in a pigsty, destroys the dinosaurs at a museum and ends up as the first monkey in space. [Houghton Mifflin Company, 1976, hardcover ISBN: 0395169739]

- "Curious George Gets a Medal," *Curious George, Houghton Mifflin Company,* http://www.houghtonmifflinbooks.com/features/cgsite/cgtgpdfs/cgtgmedal.pdf (17 June 2003).
Use this activity for writing a paragraph about someone who deserves to get a medal. A portion of the activity sheet has a space for designing a medal. This would make a good Mother's Day or Father's Day activity.

Curious George Learns the Alphabet

> Annotation: George's friend, the man with the yellow hat, teaches George to read. [Houghton Mifflin Company, 1976, hardcover ISBN: 0395160316]

- "Curious George Learns the Alphabet," *Curious George, Houghton Mifflin Company*, http://www.houghtonmifflinbooks.com/features/cgsite/cgtgpdfs/cgtglearnsalpha. pdf (17 June 2003).
  This activity from the Curious George web site can be used to strengthen phonics skills.

Curious George Takes a Job

> Annotation: Curious George continues his antics when he manages to escape from the zoo, gets a job, goes to the hospital, and ends up as a movie star. [Houghton Mifflin Company, 1976, hardback ISBN: 0395150868]

- Shinn, Kathy. "Labor Day Tools," *LessonPlansPage.com*, http://www.lessonplanspage.com/SSLaborDayToolsK2.htm (17 June 2003).
  This lesson plan is a good extension for the book.

- Tiffany. "Sample Picture Book: Curious George Takes a Job," *LearningShouldBeFun.com*, http://www.learningshouldbefun.com/samplepicturebook.html (17 June 2003).
  This community helpers unit is a good extension for the book. A mobile activity accompanies the lesson.

Classroom Center Ideas

Curious George Arts and Crafts Center

Materials: computer with Internet access, printer, crayons or colored pencils, scissors, glue

- Go to *DLTK's Book Breaks*:
  http://www.dltk-kids.com/books/curiousgeorge.html
  Select from coloring pages, a craft project, and a bookmark.

- For another bookmark design, go to the *County of Los Angeles Public Library* site:
  http://www.colapublib.org/children/kids/wild/arts/bookmark/george. html

Curious George Activity Center

Materials: computer with Internet access, printer, collection of Curious George books, pencils, crayons or colored pencils

- Students read the *KidsReads.com* Fast Facts Sheet about Curious George:
  http://www.kidsreads.com/series/series-curious-george-facts.asp

- Students read several of the Curious George books, then visit *KidsReads.com* to take the online Curious George Trivia Quiz:
  http://www.kidsreads.com/funstuff/trivia/curious-george-triv.asp

- Students complete the Curious George Word Scramble from *KidsReads.com*:
  http://www.kidsreads.com/wordscrambles/word-curious-george.asp

- Send a Curious George e-greeting card from the *Houghton Mifflin* site:
  http://www.houghtonmifflinbooks.com/features/cgsite/ecard.shtml

- Select from dozens of reproducible activities from the "Educators and Librarians Activity Time" pages from the *Houghton Mifflin Curious George* web site:
  http://www.houghtonmifflinbooks.com/features/cgsite/teacheracttime.shtml

- Select from numerous games, puzzles, coloring sheets, and activities from Games and Fun pages on the *Houghton Mifflin Curious George* web site:
  http://www.houghtonmifflinbooks.com/features/cgsite/gamesandfun.shtml

- Print Curious George bookmarks for students:
  http://www.houghtonmifflinbooks.com/features/cgsite/partykitpdfs/cgbookmark.pdf

- Print Curious George name tags for students:
  http://www.houghtonmifflinbooks.com/features/cgsite/partykitpdfs/cgpartynametags.pdf

- After studying Curious George and reading the books, have a Curious George Birthday Party, complete with invitations:
  http://www.houghtonmifflinbooks.com/features/cgsite/partykitpdfs/cgpartyinvitation.pdf

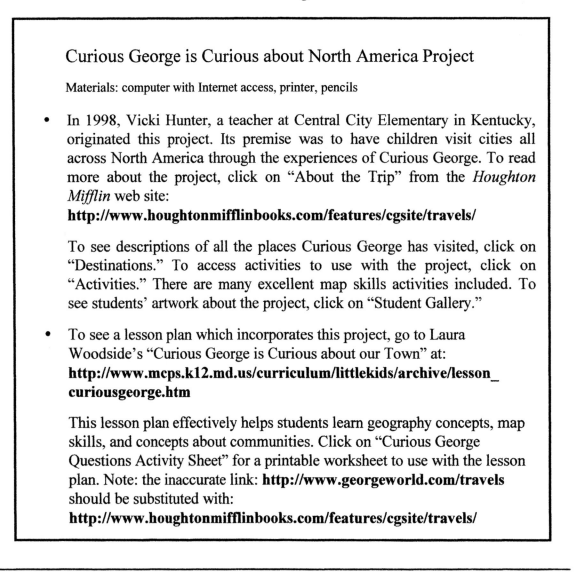

Curious George is Curious about North America Project

Materials: computer with Internet access, printer, pencils

- In 1998, Vicki Hunter, a teacher at Central City Elementary in Kentucky, originated this project. Its premise was to have children visit cities all across North America through the experiences of Curious George. To read more about the project, click on "About the Trip" from the *Houghton Mifflin* web site:
  http://www.houghtonmifflinbooks.com/features/cgsite/travels/

  To see descriptions of all the places Curious George has visited, click on "Destinations." To access activities to use with the project, click on "Activities." There are many excellent map skills activities included. To see students' artwork about the project, click on "Student Gallery."

- To see a lesson plan which incorporates this project, go to Laura Woodside's "Curious George is Curious about our Town" at:
  http://www.mcps.k12.md.us/curriculum/littlekids/archive/lesson_ curiousgeorge.htm

  This lesson plan effectively helps students learn geography concepts, map skills, and concepts about communities. Click on "Curious George Questions Activity Sheet" for a printable worksheet to use with the lesson plan. Note: the inaccurate link: **http://www.georgeworld.com/travels** should be substituted with:
  http://www.houghtonmifflinbooks.com/features/cgsite/travels/

© Permissions

⊠ Making Contact

Houghton Mifflin Company
Trade and Reference Division
Editorial and Sales Offices
222 Berkeley Street
Boston, Massachusetts 02116

The William Steig Web Site

William Steig

http://www.williamsteig.com

Description of Site

The author's web site offers a vast amount of knowledge about the author, his life, and his works. There is abundant biographical information about the author from reprints of articles found in other sources. The *Awards* pages include a chronological list of the numerous awards Mr. Steig has received for his books. The *Bookshelf* portion of the web site has details about the books, glorious, full image sample pages from the books, and reviews. The web site is a tribute to Mr. Steig and his body of work.

Best of Site: The Reading Guides

Four reading guides are included on the web site. These guides, written by Sue Ornstein, include suggestions for using the books in a classroom setting. They offer good extension activities for the themes expressed in the stories and suggest cross-curricular tie-ins. For example, the guide for *Doctor DeSoto* expands on dental care and has a link to the Colgate-Palmolive web site. The guide for *Brave Irene* correlates with a study of weather. The *Amos & Boris* guide brings in a study of mammals and links to the Monterey Bay Aquarium and the Birmingham Zoo web sites. The guides also suggest ways to analyze the character traits of the main characters in the stories, they offer comparison and contrasting activities, and they provide problem-solving activities.

Lesson plan ideas in this chapter...	Special features of site...
◆ *Brave Irene*	◆ Biographical articles
◆ *Doctor DeSoto*	◆ Sample pages from the books
◆ *Shrek!*	◆ Caldecott Award Acceptance
◆ *Sylvester and the Magic Pebble*	Speech

About the Author

William Steig began his career as a political cartoonist during the Depression and became famous while creating cartoons and covers for *The New Yorker* magazine. Not until later in life, when most people are contemplating retirement, did Mr. Steig begin to write children's picture books and novels. His books for children became overnight sensations and have won him numerous awards, including the Christopher Award for *Dominic*, the Caldecott Award for *Sylvester and the Magic Pebble*, the Newbery Honor Award for *Abel's Island*, and the Caldecott Honor Award for *Doctor DeSoto*. His book *Shrek!* has become a major motion picture. Mr. Steig combines humor with themes that borrow from human nature and common childhood fears. He uses magic and transformation in his stories, much like traditional fairy tales. His works are indeed contemporary fairy tales that delight both children and adults. The world of children's literature is a richer place thanks to the artistic and creative genius of Mr. Steig.

Online Author Studies

- "About William Steig," *William Steig*, http://www.williamsteig.com/williamsteig.htm (15 June 2003). [reprint from "Something About the Author," volume 111, edited by Alan Hedblad, *The Gale Group*, 2000.]
  This lengthy biography is on the author's web site and has links to four other articles about the author.

- "EPA's Top 100 Authors: William Steig," Educational Paperback Association, http://www.edupaperback.org/showauth.cfm?authid=43 (17 June 2003).
  This biography delves into Mr. Steig's childhood and young adulthood and gives glimpses into the events that helped shaped his writing career.

- Koch, John. "The Interview: William Steig," *The Boston Globe Magazine*, http://www.boston.com/globe/magazine/6-22/interview/ (15 June 2003).
  This site gives a candid interview with the author.

- "William Steig," *Kidsreads.com*, http://www.kidsreads.com/authors/au-steig-william.asp (15 June 2003).
  This brief biography is accompanied by links to a *Shrek!* word search and *Shrek!* trivia quiz.

Lesson Plan Ideas

Brave Irene

> Annotation: Irene, the daughter of a dressmaker, decides to deliver a dress to the Duchess for her mother, who is ill. She has to trek through a blizzard but perseveres through many obstacles along her way. Her bravery is rewarded when she reaches the Duchess' palace. [Farrar, Straus, and Giroux, 1986, hardcover ISBN: 0374309477]

- "Brave Irene," *Alta Murrieta Elementary School, Murrieta, CA*, http://www.murrieta.k12.ca.us/alta/grade3/braveirene/activities.html (16 June 2003).

  This site has excellent extension activities that include six online activities and seven printable activities to use with the story. The online activities include Rags to Riches, Hangman, Concentration, Flashcards, Matching, and a Word Search. The printable activities include writing prompts, a script for a class play, a synonym activity, verb activity, noun activities, and a crossword puzzle.

- Di Piazza, Janine. "TeacherView: Brave Irene," *Education Place, Houghton Mifflin Company*, http://www.eduplace.com/tview/pages/b/Brave_Irene_William_Steig.html (16 June 2003).

  Scroll down the page for this TeacherView. Three activities are suggested to use with the story: practice with sequence of events, a lesson on adjectives, and a writing activity about bravery and perseverance.

- Liauba, Julie. "Brave Irene," *St. Agnes School, Ft. Wright, KY*, http://members.aol.com/Winter2nd/agnes.htm (16 June 2003).

  This classroom site has student letters to Irene, letters to William Steig, letters from the Duchess to Mrs. Bobbin, revised endings to the book, and 5W poems (who, what, when, where, why). Use these examples to teach letter writing, 5W poetry, or other creative writing activities.

- "Brave Irene," *BookPals.net*, http://www.bookpals.net/storyline/braveirene/ (16 June 2003).

  On the left side of the screen, view former Vice President Al Gore read aloud from the story. (QuickTime, Windows Media, or RealPlayer required.) On the right side of the screen, see a lesson plan for the story with activities, a biographical sketch, and a story element chart.

Doctor DeSoto

> Annotation: This Newbery Honor Award book is the story of a dentist who is famous for treating large animals with their dental problems. One day, a fox with a terrible toothache comes to the dentist for help. Unfortunately for the dentist, the fox plans to eat him after his tooth is fixed. [Farrar, Straus, and Giroux, 1982, hardback ISBN: 0374318034]

- "Doctor DeSoto," *Anonymous*,
  http://www.lexington1.net/lv/sges/hp.nsf/Files/literary/$FILE/DrDeSoto.htm (17 June 2003).
  This page posts vocabulary words and definitions found in the story. Use these in a thesaurus or dictionary activity.

- "Moving Along with Simple Machines," *Henry County Public Schools, GA*,
  http://www.henry.k12.ga.us/cur/simp-mach/week-2.htm (17 June 2003).
  This ingenious lesson integrates the study of simple machines with literature. Scroll down to Day 9 to see the activities for *Doctor DeSoto*. Included is a link to a Scavenger Hunt Sheet. The story depicts the pulley and lever.

- Spatz, Anne. "Doctor DeSoto Character Pillows," *Emerson Public Schools, NJ*,
  http://www.emerson.k12.nj.us/staff/aspatz/000000000280.html (17 June 2003).
  This unique idea is presented as a gallery of photographs depicting students' creations. The pillows can be used to dramatize the story.

Sylvester and the Magic Pebble

> Annotation: This Caldecott Award-winning book is the story of Sylvester, a donkey, who finds a magic pebble one day. He suddenly finds himself face to face with a ferocious lion and impulsively wishes he could be a rock. His wish comes true. His parents are heartbroken until one day they decide to move on with their life and go on a picnic. [Simon & Schuster, 1988, hardcover ISBN: 067166154X]

- Burr, Carol, Valerie McAnally, and Shannon Taylor. "Teacher CyberGuide: Sylvester and the Magic Pebble," *Metro-Nashville School System, Nashville, TN*,
  http://www.nashville.k12.tn.us/CyberGuides/Sylvester/tch.html (16 June 2003).
  This CyberGuide, intended for grade three, can be adapted for use with younger grades. It incorporates the study of rocks as an extension to the story. It has good activities and links to rock-related web sites.

- Deb. "Sylvester and the Magic Pebble," *Teachers.net*,
    http://teachers.net/lessons/posts/1270.html (17 June 2003).
  This integrated lesson plan has many activities of which the cause and effect activity and the mapping activity are notable.

- Dye, Renee. "Rocks and Sylvester and the Magic Pebble," *LessonPlansPage.com*,
    EdScope, L. L. C., http://www.lessonplanspage.com/ScienceLARocks-
    SylvesterMagicPebbleCritique12.htm (16 June 2003).
  This lesson plan uses the story to effectively introduce various kinds of rocks to younger students.

Classroom Center Ideas

Creative Writing Center

Materials: computer with Internet access, printer, paper, pencils, crayons or colored pencils

- View the following web sites for examples of stories about bravery:

  Mrs. Fuller's class stories, "Brave Stories" (*Alta Murrieta Elementary School, Murrieta, CA*):
  http://www.murrieta.k12.ca.us/alta/dfuller/2001/brave.html

  Mrs. Greenberg's class stories, "Brave Irene" (*Francis W. Parker School, Chicago, IL*): **http://www.kids-learn.org/frosty/parker.htm**

  Susan Silverman's class stories, "Frosty Readers Project: Brave Irene" (*Clinton Avenue Elementary School, Port Jefferson Station, NY*):
  http://www.kids-learn.org/frosty/silverman.htm

  Cheryl Singer's class stories, "Brave Memories" (*Comsewogue Schools, NY*):
  http://comsewogue.k12.ny.us/~csinger/projects/braveirene/brave irene.htm

  Mrs. Underwood's class stories, "Brave Stories" (*St. Thomas More School, Baton Rouge, LA)*:
  http://www.thomasmoresch.org/Underwood/BraveStories/brave.html

- Go to Cheryl Singer's "My Brave Memory Worksheet" (*Comsewogue Schools, NY*):
  http://comsewogue.k12.ny.us/~csinger/projects/braveirene/worksheet. htm
  Print and use as a guide for students to write their own stories of bravery.

Shrek! Center

Materials: computer with Internet access, Macromedia Shockwave plug-in, RealPlayer or Windows Media to view multimedia clips, pencils, *Shrek!* Characterization Worksheet, a copy of the book *Shrek!*

- To read about the book and the movie, go to:
  http://www.kidsreads.com/features/0522-shrek.asp

- To view the movie's production photos, go to:
  http://www.upcomingmovies.com/shrek.html
  From the main menu, click on *Production Photos*. Then, click on the first thumbnail sketch to enlarge, thereafter click on "Next Photo." Students can view the movie photos and read the captions. Note to teachers: reduce the page image by dragging the right-hand margin to the left to eliminate the advertising window.

- To view the official movie site, go to: **http://www.shrek.com/**
  Here, one can go *Behind the Scenes* to find information about the cast, crew, the story, the technology used to make the movie, go to *Trailers* to view video clips, *Meet the Characters*, go to *Games* to play *Shrek!* Concentration and use online paint tools to color S*hrek!* Coloring Pages, and view the *Image Gallery*.

- To take a *Shrek!* Trivia Quiz and *Shrek!* Word Scramble, go to *KidsReads.com*:
  http://www.kidsreads.com/funstuff/trivia/shrek-triv.asp
  http://www.kidsreads.com/wordscrambles/word-shrek.asp

© Permissions

Farrar, Straus and Giroux
19 Union Square West
New York, NY 10003
FAX: 212-633-9385
e-mail: "mailto:Rights@fsgee.com"

✉ Making Contact

William Steig, c/o Children's Marketing Department
Farrar, Straus, and Giroux
19 Union Square West
New York, NY 10003

Shrek! Characterization Activity

Name _____

Directions: Write four adjectives about each of the main characters, then write a sentence about the character.

Shrek

_____   _____

_____   _____

_____

Donkey

_____   _____

_____   _____

_____

Fiona

_____   _____

_____   _____

_____

Farquaad

_____   _____

_____   _____

_____

Dragon

_____   _____

_____   _____

_____

The Rosemary Wells Web Site

The World of Rosemary Wells

http://www.rosemarywells.com

Description of Site

Welcome to the world of Max and Ruby. Ms. Wells has created a bright, colorful, and appealing site with sections specifically designed for parents, teachers, and kids. The inviting home page has animated book covers of favorite titles and leads the reader into the realm of some of the most popular picture books for children. The *Meet Rosemary Wells* section has autobiographical information about the author. The *Book List* section gives an extensive list of the author's works and reviews of many of her works. The *Fun with Max and Ruby* section has coloring pages and bunny money printables. The *For Parents and Teachers* section contains important information about reading to young children.

Best of Site: *Read to Your Bunny*

This section is a must-read for educators, parents, and caregivers. It is a reprint of *The Most Important Twenty Minutes of Your Day*, an excerpt from the author's book *Read to Your Bunny* (Scholastic Press, c1997, ISBN 059030284). It also has a link to the author's latest speech entitled *Children At Risk*, which discusses the premise that "the child who sits in a reader's lap is more privileged than the child who is given fancy computer games, state-of-the-art sports equipment, designer clothes." There is another link in this section outlining a read aloud program called *Read to Your Bunny* and information from experts about the importance of reading aloud.

Lesson plan ideas in this chapter...	Special features of site...
◆ *Bunny Money*	◆ Printable Bunny Money
◆ *Bunny Cakes*	◆ Interactive Matching Game
◆ *Max and Ruby's Midas*	◆ Coloring Pages

About the Author

Born in New York City and spending her childhood years in New Jersey, Rosemary Wells grew up in a house filled with literature and music. Her mother was a dancer with the Russian Ballet and her father was a playwright and actor. Her grandmother took her on many trips to New York City to visit the theater and museums. At the very young age of two, Ms. Wells began to show an interest in drawing. She later pursued her talent at the Museum School in Boston, but left without graduating, married, and moved to New York City where she began her career as a textbook designer. Soon after beginning her job, she wrote her first children's book, an illustrated edition of Gilbert and Sullivan's *I Have a Song to Sing-o*. Ms. Wells' career spans over thirty years and she has written over sixty books. She is the recipient of numerous awards for children's literature. Her talent lies not only in her lively illustrations, but in her ability to build animal characters that have the same feelings, desires, and disappointments of children everywhere.

Online Author Studies

- "Author Site: Rosemary Wells," *Penguin Group (USA) Inc.*,
  http://www.penguinputnam.com/Author/AuthorFrame?0000027335
  (18 April 2003).
  This site has a lengthy biography, an interview with the author, and a bibliography of her work.

- Corley, Diane Brazell. "Rosemary Wells," *Young Bookworm University, Garden Lakes Elementary School*,
  http://coe.west.asu.edu/students/dcorley/authors/Wells.htm
  (17 April 2003).
  This engaging site is designed for primary children and guides them as they explore the author and her works.

- "EPA's Top 100 Authors: Rosemary Wells," *Educational Paperback Association*,
  http://www.edupaperback.org/showauth.cfm?authid=163 (18 April 2003).
  This site has a detailed autobiography.

- "Rosemary Wells's Biography," *Scholastic, Inc.*,
  http://www2.scholastic.com/teachers/authorsandbooks/authorstudies/authorhome.
  jhtml?authorID=97&collateralID=5301 (18 April 2003).
  This site has a biography, interview, and a booklist of the author's works.

- Silvey, Anita. "Horn Book Radio Interview: Rosemary Wells," *Horn Book Virtual History Exhibit*, http://www.hbook.com/exhibit/wellsradio.html (17 April 2003).
  This site has an informative interview with the author with the option to listen to it.

Lesson Plan Ideas

Bunny Cakes

> Annotation: For Grandma's birthday, Max wants to make her an earthworm birthday cake. His sister Ruby is going to make an angel surprise cake with raspberry fluff icing. Read to see how Max "helps" Ruby with the baking. [Penguin Putnam Books for Young Readers, 1999, ISBN: 0670886866]

- Hooper, Julie. "Bunny Cakes and Graphing," *Technology Learning Community, Winthrop University,* http://coe.winthrop.edu/tlc/lesson_plans/Hooper/bunny_cakes.htm (18 April 2003).
  This lesson plan provides step-by-step instructions for using a spreadsheet program to enter data about the cakes in the story and making a graph from the data.

- Nicole. "Online Bunny Cakes Quiz," *Quia Corporation,* http://quia.com/pop/3576.html (17 April 2003).
  Students will enjoy taking this interactive quiz while getting feedback on their answers.

- Cooking Activity: Make Max's Earthworm Cake or Ruby's Angel Surprise Cake with Raspberry Fluff Icing from devil's food and angel food cake mixes, gummy worms, red hots, raspberry icing or whipped topping tinted pink.

Max and Ruby's Midas

> Annotation: Ruby decides to cure Max of eating too many sweets. She reads Max a Greek myth about young Prince Midas who uses magic to turn healthy food into delicious desserts. But when Midas accidentally transforms his mother into a dessert he realizes that there can be too much of a good thing. [Penguin Putnam Books for Young Readers, 2000, paperback ISBN: 0140566678]

- "Eat the Five Food Group Way! Activities," *Nutrition Explorations,* http://www.nutritionexplorations.com/educators/lessons/five-foods/fivefoods-activities.asp (30 June 2003).
  This site has many good activities and worksheets to use in a study about nutrition.

- Griffin, Amy. "Food Pyramid Unit," *Nottoway County Public Schools, VA*, http://www.geocities.com/Athens/Troy/5059/food.html (30 June 2003). This site has photographs of students' activities to learn about the food pyramid.

- Smith, Katy. "TeacherView: Max and Ruby's Midas," *Education Place, Houghton Mifflin Company*, http://www.eduplace.com/tview/tviews/m/maxandrubysmidas.html (18 April 2003). This lesson idea includes activities with the food pyramid and reinforces healthy eating concepts.

- "Unique Health and Nutrition Worksheets and Other Activities," *National Heart Savers Association,* http://www.heartsavers.org/CurriculumList.htm (30 June 2003). This is a good resource for activity sheets, games, and puzzles about nutrition.

- Read more about nutrition and how to read food labels from *Kids World*: http://www.ncagr.com/cyber/kidswrld/nutrition/

- Play the Food Guide Pyramid Game from *KidsHealth*: http://kidshealth.org/kid/stay_healthy/food/pyramid.html

- Print a chart to track what you eat from the *USDA's Food Guide Pyramid*: http://www.usda.gov/cnpp/KidsPyra/LittlePyr.pdf

- Read more about the food pyramid at the *USDA* site: http://www.nal.usda.gov:8001/py/pmap.htm

Bunny Money

> Annotation: Max and Ruby go shopping for Grandma's birthday and spend so much money on other things (thanks to Max's antics) that they just barely have enough money left for gifts. [Penguin Putnam Books for Young Readers, 2000, paperback ISBN: 014056750X]

- "Between the Lions Printable Money," *PBSkids.org*, http://pbskids.org/lions/printables/misc/money.html (17 April 2003). Use these printables for hands-on classroom activities with money.

- Blumenthal, Sarah and Amy Standridge. "Money Lesson Plan," *LessonPlansPage.com*, http://www.lessonplanspage.com/MathMoney2.htm (3 May 2003).
  This lesson plan will help reinforce money concepts with primary children.

- Deb. "Math Lessons About Money," *Teachers.net*, http://teachers.net/lessons/posts/1491.html (30 June 2003).
  This is a comprehensive unit to teach money skills to young children.

- Hernandez, Beverly. "Penny Day," *Homeschooling, About, Inc.*, http://homeschooling.miningco.com/library/blmay23a.htm (30 June 2003).
  This is a collection of lessons about pennies.

- "Lesson: Bunny Money," *KidEConBooks, Inc.*, http://www.kidseconbooks.com/html/bunny_money.html (21 April 2003).
  This site has excellent comprehension questions and answers to use with the book.

- Wells, Rosemary. "Fun with Max and Ruby: Make Bunny Money," *The World of Rosemary Wells*, http://www.rosemarywells.com (17 April 2003).
  This page from the author's web site has printable bunny money to use with classroom activities.

- For more information on money and interactive games, go to these sites:
  Money Central for Kids, http://www.bep.treas.gov/kids/start.html
  U.S. Mint for Kids, http://www.usmint.gov/kids
  Money Experience for Kids, http://www.edu4kids.com/money
  KidsBank.com, http://www.kidsbank.com/
  U.S. Treasury for Kids, http://www.ustreas.gov/kids
  Alfy's Picks for Money,
  http://www.alfy.com/teachers/teach/thematic_units/Money/Money_1.asp

- Get Money Worksheets at *Money Instructor*, http://www.moneyinstructor.com/

- Bunny Lunch Menu Activity Center
  On a chart, cut out pictures of lunch menu items and label their prices to display at the center. Use a toy cash register as a prop. With partners, students will take turns ordering from the menu and being the cashier. Using the *Bunny Lunch Menu Activity* sheet, have students "order" lunch, calculate how much they will spend, decide how much money to give the "cashier," and calculate how much change they should receive. Use real Bunny Money (available from the Rosemary Wells web site) and printable coins from *PBSkids.org's Between the Lions* Printable Money: http://pbskids.org/lions/printables/misc/money.html.

Classroom Center Ideas

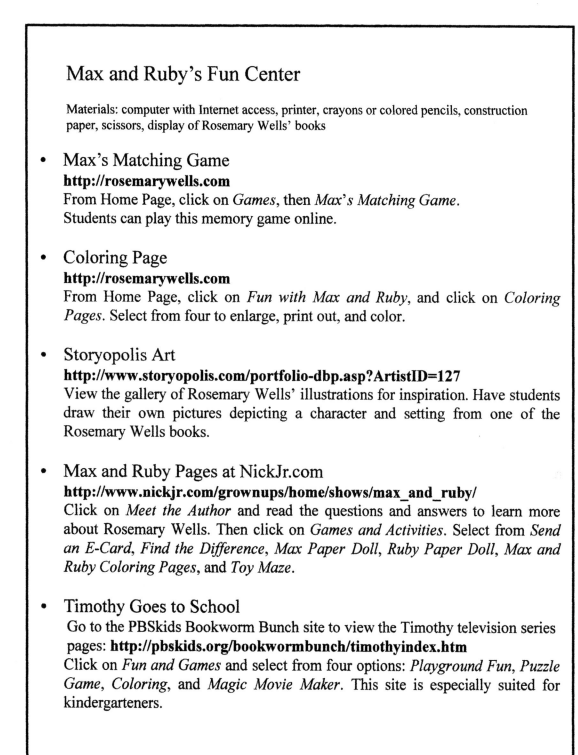

Max and Ruby's Fun Center

Materials: computer with Internet access, printer, crayons or colored pencils, construction paper, scissors, display of Rosemary Wells' books

- Max's Matching Game
  http://rosemarywells.com
  From Home Page, click on *Games*, then *Max's Matching Game*.
  Students can play this memory game online.

- Coloring Page
  http://rosemarywells.com
  From Home Page, click on *Fun with Max and Ruby*, and click on *Coloring Pages*. Select from four to enlarge, print out, and color.

- Storyopolis Art
  http://www.storyopolis.com/portfolio-dbp.asp?ArtistID=127
  View the gallery of Rosemary Wells' illustrations for inspiration. Have students draw their own pictures depicting a character and setting from one of the Rosemary Wells books.

- Max and Ruby Pages at NickJr.com
  http://www.nickjr.com/grownups/home/shows/max_and_ruby/
  Click on *Meet the Author* and read the questions and answers to learn more about Rosemary Wells. Then click on *Games and Activities*. Select from *Send an E-Card, Find the Difference, Max Paper Doll, Ruby Paper Doll, Max and Ruby Coloring Pages*, and *Toy Maze*.

- Timothy Goes to School
  Go to the PBSkids Bookworm Bunch site to view the Timothy television series pages: **http://pbskids.org/bookwormbunch/timothyindex.htm**
  Click on *Fun and Games* and select from four options: *Playground Fun, Puzzle Game, Coloring*, and *Magic Movie Maker*. This site is especially suited for kindergarteners.

Bunny Lunch Menu Activity
Use with the book *Bunny Money* by Rosemary Wells

Name _____

Select 5 items from the following menu:

◆	Grilled Cheese Sandwich	$1.50
◆	Hamburger	$2.10
◆	Hot Dog	$1.50
◆	Peanut Butter and Jelly Sandwich	$1.75
◆	Potato Chips	$ .50
◆	French Fries	$ .75
◆	Chocolate Chip Cookie	$ .50
◆	Pudding	$ .50
◆	Coconut Cupcake	$ .50
◆	Soda	$ .75
◆	Banana Shake	$1.25
◆	Lemonade	$ .75
◆	Apple Juice	$ .75

List Your Choices: Write the Prices:

_____   _____

_____   _____

_____   _____

_____   _____

_____   _____

Add the prices of your choices together: _____

My total bill is: $_____

How much money will you give the cashier?   _____

How much change will you get back?   _____

Timothy Goes to School Center

Materials: computer with Internet Access, printer, crayons or colored pencils

- Bookmark this site from *The Bookworm Bunch, PBSkids.org*:
  http://pbskids.org/bookwormbunch/timothyindex.htm

- Click on "Fun and Games" to play these interactive games:
  Magic Movie Maker
  Online Coloring
  Puzzle Game (requires Flash plug-in)
  Playground Fun

- Teachers: see the "Show Info" section to learn about this television series created from the Rosemary Wells books and to see descriptions of the episodes.

© Permissions

The *Read to Your Bunny* cover art and essay from the book, published by
Scholastic Press, are available to use and print for reading and literacy initiatives only.

⊠ Making Contact

Write to Rosemary Wells:
c/o Penguin Putnam Books for Young Readers
345 Hudson Street
New York, NY 10014

E-mail:
mail@rosemarywells.com

Children's Picture Book Illustration

The illustrator's craft is worthy of further discussion. The following web sites have been selected for use by teachers, librarians, and students to learn more about the processes involved in book illustration and book making. These sites have been chosen for their particular appeal to younger students as they learn more about picture book design and production. There is also a section on lesson plans for educators to help teach these topics to children.

What Is a Picture Book?

- "What is a Picture Book?" http://www.libsci.sc.edu/Hayne/Picture%20books.pdf (19 June 2003).
  This web site may be viewed as HTML or in PDF format. If enlarged, it can be viewed as a slide show to help students learn what makes a book a picture book. It also gives a brief history of children's picture book illustration and discusses the Caldecott Award.

How a Book Is Made

- Aliki. "How a Book Is Made...," *HarperChildrens.com*, http://www.harperchildrens.com/hch/picture/features/aliki/howabook/book1.asp (19 June 2003).
  This online version of the book is in slide show format and helps students learn about the many processes in writing, illustrating, and producing a book.

- Clapp, John. "The Prince of Butterflies Process," *John Clapp Illustration*, http://www.johnclapp.com/pob/pob_process.htm (20 June 2003).
  This well-done site illustrates and describes the many steps involved in creating picture books.

- "How a Book Is Made," *Penguin Putnam UK*, http://www.penguin.co.uk/shared/SharedDisplayTable/1,,15854_1,00.html (20 June 2003).
  This slide show humorously explains the process of book making.

- "Page by Page: Creating a Children's Book," *The National Library of Canada*, http://www.nlc-bnc.ca/pagebypage/index-e.html (19 June 2003).
  This site shows how books for children are made. Using real-life examples, students will discover the step-by-step process: "starting with where the idea came from, all the way to what happens after the book is printed."

How Illustrations Are Created

- Stevens, Janet. "Making Color in Books," *Janetstevens.com*,
  http://www.janetstevens.com/graphics/ColorSeps/MakingColor.htm
  (19 June 2003).
  This section of the author/illustrator's web site gives interesting information on how picture books are designed and the process of adding colors. There is information about overlays and an interactive example showing the process.

- Stevens, Janet. "Janet Stevens," *Janetstevens.com*, http://www.janetstevens.com
  (19 June 2003).
  This award-winning author/illustrator gives a detailed description of computer generated digital art, with examples, on her web site. Click on the links for "Page Histories" digitally produced illustrations. Click on "Drawing from Props" to see one technique used in illustration. Click on "Digital Versions of a Cock-a-Doodle-Doo Page" to see the whole process unfold. Click on "FAQ" to learn more about digital art. Click on "Studio" to see individual illustration projects in different stages of production.

A Retrospective Look at Children's Book Illustration

- Amoss, John. "Part One: History of Children's Book Illustration," *The University of Georgia*, http://www.mindspring.com/~amoss/bookillustration/2history.html
  (19 June 2003).
  This concise history has many links of examples of picture book illustration from its beginnings to the present.

- Baldwin Library of Historical Children's Literature. "Cover Story,"
  Department of Special Collections, George A. Smathers Library, University of Florida, http://www.library.ubc.ca/edlib/egoffbib/ (21 June 2003).
  This is a virtual exhibit of historical book covers.

- "Canadian Children's Books 1799-1939," *Special Collections and University Archives Division, University of British Columbia Library*,
  http://www.library.ubc.ca/edlib/egoffbib/ (21 June 2003).
  View the history of Canadian children's literature, with illustrations. Click on the link "Illustrations" from the menu to access.

- "Children's Book Illustration," *Infoplease.com*,
  http://www.infoplease.com/ce6/ent/A0811852.html (19 June 2003).
  This informative site outlines the history of picture book illustration and contains links to illustrators' biographies.

- "Children's Literature and Education: Impressions of 250 Years of Printing in the Lives of Canadians," *National Library of Canada*, http://www.nlc-bnc.ca/2/10/h10-206-e.html (21 June 2003).

  This is a history of Canadian children's literature with enlargeable facsimiles of examples.

- Cotsen Children's Library. "Research Collection: Collection Highlights," *Princeton University*, http://www.princeton.edu/%7Ecotsen/research/collection_highlights.html# (21 June 2003).

  This site has enlargeable thumbnail graphics of historic examples from children's literature.

- "The Elizabeth Nesbitt Room Chapbook Collection," *Information Sciences Library, University of Pittsburgh*, http://www.library.pitt.edu/libraries/is/enroom/chapbooks/chapbookpage index.htm (21 June 2003).

  Chapbooks were very early children's books made affordable for the first time to people who previously had never been able to buy books of their own. They were also some of the first books ever published for children. Street peddlers or chapmen usually sold them. This collection is indexed by title, subject, and publisher and includes chapbooks from England, America, and Scotland in the years 1650 to 1850. Facsimiles of the covers are included and links to other sites with chapbook collections are given.

- "The Elizabeth Nesbitt Room Illustrator's Project," *Information Sciences Library, University of Pittsburgh*, http://www.library.pitt.edu/libraries/is/enroom/illustrators/index.htm (21 June 2003).

  This magnificent collection is comprised of ten special collections featuring noted children's book illustrators of the nineteenth and early twentieth centuries. The collections include biographical information, facsimiles of works, bibliographies, secondary sources, and links to related sites. The illustrators included in the collections are: Walter Crane, Beatrix Potter, Richard Doyle, Trina Schart Hyman, Kay Nielsen, Howard Pyle, Arthur Rackham, Ernest Shepard, Jesse Wilcox Smith, and Newell Convers Wyeth.

- The Elizabeth Nesbitt Room. "Preservation/Rare Books Pathfinder," *Information Sciences Library, University of Pittsburgh*, http://www.library.pitt.edu/libraries/is/enroom/pathfinder/terms. tm#hornbook (21 June 2003).

  This is an outstanding collection of examples that illustrate various terms important to the study of the history of books, publishing, book preservation, binding, paper-making, and methods of illustration. It is arranged much like a pictorial dictionary in that it lists terms alphabetically and gives enlargeable facsimiles to show examples.

- Grenby, Matthew. "The Hockliffe Project," *Department of English and Centre for Technology and the Arts, De Montfort University,* http://malkyn.hum.dmu.ac.uk:8000/AnaServer?hockliffe+0+start.anv (21 June 2003).
This impressive collection houses works from early British children's literature. Select from different categories or genres, then click on the catalog numbers to link to facsimiles of pages from early works.

- Hugh M. Morris Library. "World of the Child: Two Hundred Years of Children's Books," *Special Collections, University of Delaware Library,* http://www.lib.udel.edu/ud/spec/exhibits/child/ (20 June 2003).
This site gives a complete history of children's book illustration and children's literature with enlargeable facsimiles.

- "Illustrations by Lois Lenski," *The University of Montana Museum of Fine Arts Drawing Collection,* http://grizzly.umt.edu/partv/famus/draw/lenski/lenski.htm (21 June 2003).
Twenty-one illustrations from the Lois Lenski Collection are depicted here.

- Lowenberg, Melissa. "Alice's Adventures in Wonderland," *University of British Columbia Special Collections Division,* http://www.library.ubc.ca/spcoll/alice/index.html (21 June 2003).
This virtual exhibit, "The Alice 100 Collection," celebrates the 100th anniversary of the first publication of *Alice* in 1865.

- McKenzie, Andrea. "The Art Gallery," *University of Waterloo, Calgary,* http://arts.uwaterloo.ca/ENGL/courses/engl208c/gallery.htm (21 June 2003).
This page contains illustrations from children's magazines and books from 1870 to 1930.

- The Miriam Snow Mathis Historical Children's Literature Collection. "Digital Exhibit: Elements of Book Design and Illustration," *M. E. Grenander Department of Special Collections and Archives, University at Albany Libraries,* http://library.albany.edu/speccoll/design/ (21 June 2003).
View samples from this collection of nineteenth and early twentieth century book illustration. The captioned facsimiles can be enlarged.

- "The Morgan Collection," *The University of Melbourne,* http://www.lib.unimelb.edu.au/whatson/exhib/morgan/ex971.html (21 June 2003).
This site has a virtual exhibit of early children's books.

- "Picturing Childhood: The Evolution of the Illustrated Children's Book," *The University of California*, http://www2.library.ucla.edu/libraries/special/childhood/pictur.htm#anchor 282996 (20 June 2003).
This is a scholarly, comprehensive history of children's book illustration and children's book publishing with examples to view.

- Scott, Patrick. "Children's Literature, Chiefly from the Nineteenth Century," *Thomas Cooper Library, University of South Carolina*, http://www.sc.edu/library/spcoll/kidlit/kidlit/kidlit.html (21 June 2003).
This timeline showing the development of children's literature in history has enlargeable facsimiles of illustrations and covers.

- Touponce. "Children's Literature Lecture Notes and Slides," *Elizabeth Ball Collection, Lilly Library, Indiana University in Bloomington*, http://www.iupui.edu/~engwft/home.html (22 June 2003).
There are several links to information and images of early works in children's literature. The links include: Hornbooks, Chapbooks, Battledores, New England Primers, Orbis Pictus, Puritan Literature for Children, John Newbery, Mother Goose, Thomas Bewick, Moralists, George Cruikshank, Walter Crane, Beatrix Potter, Randolph Caldecott, Kate Greenaway, and more.

- Vandergrift, Dr. Kay E. "Facsimiles of Historical Children's Books," *Rutgers, The State University of New Jersey*, http://scils.rutgers.edu/%7Ekvander/HistoryofChildLit/facsims.html (20 June 2003).
This interesting site provides beautiful illustrations from early children's books. These pages portray the evolution of children's picture book illustration.

Media and Artistic Styles

- "The Art of Illustration," *National Library of Canada*, http://www.nlcbnc.ca/3/10/index-e.html (19 June 2003).
This is a good site to see examples of different artistic styles in picture book illustration, such as realism, cartoon art, concept books, and naive art.

- Hurst, Carol. "Looking Critically at Picture Books," *Carol Hurst's Children's Literature Site*, http://www.carolhurst.com/subjects/criticalpicture.html (19 June 2003).
This site offers activities to help students examine picture books.

- "Magic Pencil: Children's Book Illustration Today," *The British Library*, http://portico.bl.uk/whatson/exhibitions/magicpencil/highlights.html (19 June 2003).

This site lists renowned picture book illustrators and shows examples of their works, with critiques, to show why their illustrations are exemplary.

- Matulka, Denise I. "Picturing Books: A Web Site about Picture Books," *Picturing Books, Imaginarylands.org*, http://picturingbooks.imaginarylands.org (19 June 2003).

This outstanding site is a must-see web site to learn about picture books. Click on "Artistic Media" for explanations of oils, pastels, woodcuts, etc. It shows large, full-color examples of each of the media and gives a list of illustrators who use the media. Click on "Artistic Style" to learn about impressionism, folkart, surrealism, etc. and also see examples. Click on "Anatomy" to learn about bibliographic terms and parts of books. Click on "Resources" to learn about different categories of picture books. Excellent links are provided to learn more about picture books.

- Steffen, Susan Swords. "Children's Picture Book Examples," http://www.elmhurst.edu/~susanss/rutgers/susanexamples.html (19 June 2003).

This is a very good site to use with students to show different styles, media, and design elements in book illustration. A PowerPoint presentation is included.

- Vandergrift, Dr. Kay E. "Visual Interpretive Analysis of Children's Picture Book Illustration," *Rutgers, The State University of New Jersey*, http://www.scils.rutgers.edu/~kvander/Syllabus/art500.html (19 June 2003).

Although scholarly and useful in advanced studies, this part of the Vandergrift site can be used with elementary students to showcase individual illustrations from noted picture books for children. This would be very impressive if used with a LCD projector. Scroll down the page to the list of examples. Each example offers a question for students to ponder about the illustration. [Note to teachers: the first book in the list, *Amazon Diaries*, does show an illustration with nudity, which may not be appropriate for all viewers. Discretion is advised.]

Awards for Children's Book Illustration

- Association for Library Service to Children. "Welcome to the Caldecott Medal Home Page," *American Library Association*, http://www.ala.org/Content/NavigationMenu/ALSC/Awards_and_Scholarshi ps1/Literary_and_Related_Awards/Caldecott_Medal/Caldecott_Medal.htm (19 June 2003).

Learn about the prestigious award for excellence in children's picture book illustration and read about the history of the award.

- Brown, David K. "Children's Book Awards," *The Children's Literature Web Guide*, http://www.acs.ucalgary.ca/~dkbrown/awards.html (20 June 2003).

This site is "the most comprehensive guide to English-language children's book awards on the Internet."

- "Children's Book Awards," *Library Services, Rhode Island Department of Administration*, http://www.lori.state.ri.us/youthserv/awards.php (20 June 2003). This site has international, national, and association awards for children's books.

- Czeck, David. "The Caldecott Medal," http://ils.unc.edu/award/chome.html (20 June 2003).
This concise site gives information about the criteria of the award and its origins. It has a link to the official Caldecott Award web site. One link, to a biography of Randolph Caldecott, is inactive. Instead, go to Gwen and Allan Reichert's "Randolph Who?" site from the *Randolph Caldecott Society of America*, http://www.rcsamerica.com/rc.html (20 June 2003).

- "2003 Children's Literature Awards," *KidBibs.com*, http://kidbibs.com/home.htm (21 June 2003).
This site has all the latest award-winning books from many organizations.

Meet the Artists

- Children's Book Council. "Author Illustrator Archives," http://www.cbcbooks.org/html/archives.html (20 June 2003).
This site has biographies of noted illustrators with comments about their styles and preferred media. An example of their artwork is included.

- Cummings, Pat. *Talking with the Artists*, Volume 1, Simon & Schuster, library binding ISBN: 0027242455.
_____. *Talking with the Artists, Volume 2*, Simon & Schuster, library binding ISBN: 0689803109.
_____. *Talking with the Artists, Volume 3*, Houghton Mifflin, hardcover ISBN: 0395891329.
This series has conversations with contemporary illustrators.

- Cummins, Julie and Barbara Kiefer. *Wings of an Artist: Children's Book Illustrators Talk About their Art*, Harry N. Abrams, 1999, hardcover ISBN: 0810945525.
Twenty-three artists are depicted with information about their beginnings, their media preferences, and their styles. An activity guide offers activities to use in the classroom. Bonus: *Amazon.com* has enlargeable facsimiles of sample pages.

- Marcus, Leonard S. *Side by Side: Five Favorite Picture Book Teams Go to Work*, Walker and Company, 2001, hardcover ISBN: 0802787789.
Mr. Marcus portrays the life and works of notable children's author/illustrator teams. See sample pages from the book at *Amazon.com*.

_____. *Ways of Telling: Conversations on the Art of the Picture Book*, Dutton, 2002, hardcover ISBN: 0525464905.

This book gives insight into the creative process of fourteen children's authors and illustrators. See sample pages from the book at *Amazon.com*.

- Meyer, Susan E. *A Treasury of the Great Children's Book Illustrators*, Harry N. Abrams, 1987, paperback ISBN: 0810926946.

This book presents fourteen illustrators from the nineteenth and early twentieth centuries who made significant contributions to children's book illustration. Bonus: *Amazon.com* has enlargeable facsimiles of sample pages from this book.

The de Grummond Special Collections

The de Grummond Collection at the University of Southern Mississippi Libraries is one of the country's leading research centers in the field of children's literature. The collection holds the original manuscripts and illustrations of over 1200 published authors and illustrators. It also contains over 70,000 published works. To learn more about this collection, go to: http://www.lib.usm.edu/%7Edegrum/

- de Grummond Collection. "The Cinderella Project," *University of Southern Mississippi*, http://www-dept.usm.edu/~engdept/cinderella/imagesonly.html (20 June 2003).

Facsimiles of early editions of *Cinderella* are portrayed and are enlargeable.

- de Grummond Collection. "Jack and the Beanstalk and Jack the Giant Killer Project," *University of Southern Mississippi*, http://www-dept.usm.edu/~engdept/jack/inventi.htm (20 June 2003).

These amazing images from the virtual collection of early Jack and the Beanstalk books shows famous editions of the story.

- de Grummond Collection. "The Little Red Riding Hood Project," *University of Southern Mississippi*, http://www-dept.usm.edu/~engdept/lrrh/inventi.htm (20 June 2003).

Over a dozen early editions of *Little Red Riding Hood* are portrayed at this site.

- de Grummond Collection. "The Making of a Keats Picture Book," *University of Southern Mississippi*, http://www.lib.usm.edu/~degrum/keats/howto.html (19 June 2003).

This page from the special *Keats Collection* takes a step-by-step look at how a book is made.

Picture Book Museums, Galleries, and Virtual Exhibits

- Elizabeth Stone Gallery. "Fine Art of Children's Book Illustration,"
  http://www.esgallery.com/ (20 June 2003).
  Dozens of illustrators are part of this collection. Click on "Artists" to see a list with links to examples of their works. The media used is also included.

- Eric Carle Museum of Picture Book Art. "Exhibitions,"
  http://www.picturebookart.org/index.asp (19 June 2003).
  This site provides a virtual tour of picture book illustrations. The museum features three galleries dedicated to rotating exhibitions of picture book art.

- "European Picture Book Collection," *National Centre for Research in Children's Literature*, http://www.ncrcl.ac.uk/epbc/books/book_images.htm
  (21 June 2003).
  This site showcases one book from each of nineteen European countries. The book covers are depicted, translations of the text are provided, and classroom activities are included.

- Every Picture Tells a Story. "The Art of Illustration," http://www.everypicture.com/
  (20 June 2003).
  This gallery has works by Dr. Seuss, Garth Williams, David Shannon, and others.

- The Illustration Cupboard. http://www.illustrationcupboard.com/
  (20 June 2003).
  This bright, high-resolution site has works by many prominent illustrators of children's books. Click on "Current Catalog" to see a complete listing.

- "Images from the Marcia Brown Collection," *M. E. Grenander Department of Special Collections and Archives, University at Albany Libraries*,
  http://library.albany.edu/speccoll/findaids/marciaimages.htm (23 June 2003).
  View famous illustrations by this famed author/illustrator.

- "Mazza Virtual Tour," *Mazza Museum: International Art from Picture Books*,
  http://www.mazzacollection.org/virtual-tour-text2.htm (20 June 2003).
  This well-done slide show is a virtual tour of famed illustrations from the Mazza Collection. The illustrations have captions about the illustrator's techniques and style.

- Nels, Phil. "Welcome to the Crockett Johnson Homepage," *Department of English, University of Kansas*, http://www.ksu.edu/english/nelp/purple/index.html
  (30 June 2003).
  This site has biographical information about the author/illustrator, photographs, commentary on his illustration, and information about his characters.

- "Once upon a Drawing: The Picture Book Illustrations of Marcia Brown,"
  University Art Museum, University of Albany,
  http://www.albany.edu/museum/wwwmuseum/Brown/ (21 June 2003).
  View this virtual exhibit of works by renowned illustrator, Marcia Brown.

- "Our Permanent Collection," *The National Center for Children's Illustrated*
  Literature, http://www.nccil.org/collection/ (19 June 2003).
  Take a virtual tour of five illustrious picture book artists. The illustrators include
  William Joyce, Janet Stevens, Bernard Most, Deborah Nourse Lattimore, and Mike
  Wimmer. The exhibit includes dozens of enlargeable illustrations from each.

- R. Michelson Galleries."Children's Book Illustrators," *RMichelson.com,*
  http://www.rmichelson.com/childrens_books_illustrations.html (20 June 2003).
  This site displays the works of some of the premier children's book illustrators.
  Included in the collection are Dr. Seuss, Mordecai Gerstein, Maurice Sendak, Alice
  and Martin Provensen, Diane deGroat, and Trina Schart Hyman.

- StoryBookArt.com. http://www.storybookart.com/gallery.html (20 June 2003).
  View this excellent gallery of children's book art and read biographies of the artists.

- Storyopolis. "Storyopolis Book Gallery,"
  http://www.storyopolis.com/default_flash.asp (20 June 2003).
  Click on "Art Gallery" to see a complete list of illustrators and their works.

- "The Wonderful World of Pop-ups and Animated Books,"
  http://popupbooks.net/main.html (19 June 2003).
  This extraordinary site, although commercial, has close-up page samples from the top
  one hundred pop-up and animated books. Use this site as a preliminary activity for
  making pop-up books in the classroom.

- Vandergrift, Kay E. "Snow White Illustrations," *Rutgers, The State University of New*
  Jersey, http://www.scils.rutgers.edu/~kvander/swillustration.html (21 June 2003).
  Scroll down the page to find beautiful facsimiles of various illustrations from
  different works of *Snow White*. A link to the *Snow White* text is provided. This page is
  a part of the Vandergrift's *Snow White* site.

The Caldecott Medal: Teaching Resources

- Association for Library Service to Children, "Welcome to the Caldecott Medal Home Page!" *American Library Association,* http://www.ala.org/Content/NavigationMenu/ALSC/Awards_and_ Scholarships1/Literary_and_Related_Awards/Caldecott_Medal/Caldecott_ Medal.htm (22 June 2003).

  This is the official site for the Caldecott Medal. It gives background information about the award, lists winners from 1938 to the present, and gives the criteria and process for selecting the winning books.

- "The Caldecott Medal," *Embracing the Child,* http://www.eyeontomorrow.com/embracingthechild/caldecott.html#caldecott (22 June 2003).

  This would be a valuable resource to use to introduce a unit on the Caldecott Medal or as a review at the end of a unit. If projected onto a large screen for whole class viewing, the teacher can talk about the Caldecott-winning books, click on links about the authors and illustrators, and see images of the book covers. For the book, *Song of the Swallows,* by Leo Politi, be sure to click on the link to the Mission San Juan Capistrano.

- Frohardt, Darcie. *Teaching Art With Books Kids Love: Teaching Art Appreciation, Elements of Art, and Principles of Design With Award-Winning Children's Books,* Fulcrum Publishing, 1999, paperback ISBN: 1555914063.

  This book could be a good companion for any unit on the Caldecott Medal. It presents elements of art, discusses artistic styles, and uses Caldecott Medal-winning books as examples. See sample pages at *Amazon.com.*

- Marcus, Leonard S. *A Caldecott Celebration: Six Artists Share Their Paths to the Caldecott Medal,* New York: Walker and Company, 1998, hardcover ISBN: 0802786561.

  Noted children's book historian, Leonard S. Marcus, gives information about the Caldecott Medal and six Caldecott award-winning illustrators: Robert McCloskey, Marcia Brown, Maurice Sendak, William Steig, Chris Van Allsburg, and David Wiesner. Bonus: *Amazon.com* has thirteen enlargeable facsimiles of sample pages from the book.

- "Randolph Caldecott," *Elizabeth Ball Collection, Lilly Library, Indiana University in Bloomington*, http://www.iupui.edu/~engwft/caldecott.htm (22 June 2003).
  This site provides a biography of Randolph Caldecott and depicts images of his works.

- Reichert, Gwen. "Randolph Who? From Where? What Did He Do?" *The Randolph Caldecott Society of America*, http://www.rcsamerica.com/rc.html (22 June 2003).
  This site has good background information about the Caldecott Medal and provides a detailed biography of Randolph Caldecott and his contributions to children's book illustration.

- Story-Huffman, Ru. *Caldecott on the Net: Reading and Internet Activities*, Highsmith Press, 2002, paperback ISBN: 1579500765.
  Eighteen "LearningQuests" are presented in the book, with each focusing on a different Caldecott award-winning title. Children are presented with a theme, activities, Internet resources, and extended learning opportunities.

- "Welcome to the Randolph Caldecott Society UK," *Randolph Caldecott Society UK*, http://www.randolphcaldecott.org.uk/index.htm (22 June 2003).
  This society's web site has details about the artist's life, his works, and his accomplishments in the field of illustration. There are links to graphics of his works.

Collective Lesson Plans for a Caldecott Unit

- Bafile, Cara. "Kudos by Kiddos," *Education World, Inc.*, http://www.education-world.com/a_lesson/02/lp288-02.shtml (21 June 2003).
  This clever lesson plan has students designing a new award for a children's book, selecting a book to receive the award, creating a "medal" for the book jacket, and writing an explanation of the award and why the book has earned it. Although intended for older students, this lesson can easily be adapted for younger students.

- Johnson, Beverly, "Caldecott and Newbery Award Winning Books,"
  The WebQuest Page, Educational Technology Department, San Diego State University, http://edservices.aea7.k12.ia.us/edtech/teacherpages/bjohnson/index.html (21 June 2003).
  For primary grades, use the Caldecott portion of this webquest to help students learn about award-winning picture books.

- Kerby, Mona. "Caldecott Books," *Mona Kerby's Reading Corner*,
    http://www.carr.lib.md.us/read/caldecott.htm (22 June 2003).
    This is another good site to project onto a large screen for whole class viewing. Introduce the Caldecott Medal winners by decade. Read reviews and see images of the book covers.

- Ross, Jan. "Learning About Caldecott Books," *Dixie Elementary Magnet School, Lexington, KY*, http://www.dixie.fayette.k12.ky.us/LibSkills/libskill2.8.htm
    (22 June 2003).
    This is a nine-week unit which presents the Caldecott Medal winners and the Honor books as well as information about the award and Randolph Caldecott. There are links to nine pages of Caldecott cards, which show images of the books. It culminates by having students create quilt squares using a software paint program. This would be an excellent library media unit.

- Sample Curriculum and Plans for Education (SCoPE). "Unit Plan for Caldecotts," *State of Michigan*, http://www.michigan.gov/scope/0,1607,
    7-155-10710_10733_10735-39153--,00.html (20 June 2003).
    This site has eleven lesson plans for individual Caldecott Medal books. The plans are for the primary grades and span the years 1942 to 2001. One of the lessons includes a collection of Caldecott favorites.

- Thornton, Jerilyn. "Learning About Caldecott Winners," *Teachers.net*,
    http://www.teachers.net/lessons/posts//1360.html (23 June 2003).
    This is a good approach to teaching the Caldecott award books in three sessions.

- Tonningsen, Kirsten. "Caldecott Contenders 2002," *Riverdale Grade School, OR*,
    http://www.riverdale.k12.or.us/~ktonning/library/caldecott02.htm
    (22 June 2003).
    This imaginative idea is a wonderful way to involve students in a mock election process to select a Caldecott Medal winner from the nominated selections. View other years' contests, as well. There are book cover images, photographs of students during the activity, and students' artwork to accompany the site. An explanation of the Caldecott Award is provided. Is there a 2003 and 2004 site on the way?

Lesson Plans for Individual Caldecott Medal Winners

Every effort has been made to evaluate and include the best lesson plans found during research. Only lesson plans for primary grades have been included unless intermediate grade plans can be easily adapted for lower grades. In some cases, the plans have inactive links. They were included if the overall lesson plan was found to be beneficial in the classroom in spite of a few broken links. Sites with many broken links have not been included.

2003 *My Friend Rabbit*
by Eric Rohmann

- Lamb, Annette and Nancy Smith. "Caldecott Connections: My Friend Rabbit," *Literature Learning Ladders*, *EduScapes.com*, http://eduscapes.com/caldecott/03a.htm (22 June 2003).

This web project suggests several extension activities to use with the book, such as writing news stories, researching rabbits, and learning more about the author. There are many excellent links for young children to explore web sites that relate to the story.

2002 *The Three Pigs*
by David Wiesner

- Smith, Nancy. "Caldecott Connections: The Three Pigs," *Literature Learning Ladders*, *EduScapes.com*, http://eduscapes.com/caldecott/02a.htm (22 June 2003).

This web-based lesson has links to many sites with other versions of the story, information about the author/illustrator, factual information about pigs, and online games and activities.

2001 *So You Want to Be President?*
illustrated by David Small, text by Judith St. George

- Blair, Jill. "So You Want to Be President?" *Reading to Learn*, http://www.auburn.edu/~murraba/elucid/blairrl.html (26 June 2003).

This imaginative activity assigns each student or group of students one page in the book to summarize and present to the class. The focus of the lesson is the main idea.

- Gomez, Rebecca. "So You Want to Be President," *Scholastic, Inc.*, http://www2.scholastic.com/teachers/authorsandbooks/teachingwithbooks/ producthome.jhtml?productID=12812&collateralID=9909&displayName= Teaching+Plan (21 June 2003).
  This site has a link to a teaching plan, which can be adapted for lower grade levels to teach about our country's presidents. This is a good activity to teach beginning research skills.

- Horgeshimer, Sheryl. "So You Want to Be President?: A Social Studies WebQuest," http://coe.west.asu.edu/students/shorgeshimer/webpage/preswebquest.html (22 June 2003).
  This webquest can be adapted to use with younger students. Many links are included to extend the story and learn more about presidents, the White House, and elections.

- Lamb, Annette and Nancy Smith. "Caldecott Connections: So You Want to Be President?" *Literature Learning Ladders, EduScapes.com,* http://eduscapes.com/caldecott/01a.htm (22 June 2003).
  This lesson plan suggests that students use the World Wide Web to explore presidents and learn more about the author and illustrator. There are many good links to the web to extend the story.

- "President's Picture Book," *Education World, Inc*, http://www.education-world.com/a_lesson/01-1/lp223_05.shtml (21 June 2003).
  Use this lesson plan after reading aloud from the book. Students will create illustrations with captions about presidents to be compiled into a class book. The plan includes links to websites about presidents.

- "So You Want to Be President?" *TeacherVision.com, Family Education Network, Inc.*, http://www.teachervision.com/lesson-plans/lesson-5241.html (22 June 2003).
  Ten ideas are presented here to extend the story and include researching presidents and finding the presidents' birthplaces on a map of the United States.

- "So You Want to Be President?" *TeacherVision.com, Family Education Network, Inc.*, http://www.teachervision.com/lesson-plans/lesson-6684.html (22 June 2003).
  This is another good site with helpful links to use with the story and learn more about the author. There is a Venn diagram activity, a letter writing activity, and links to sites about presidents.

- "So You Want to Be President? Classroom Activity" *Trumpet Club,* http://trumpetclub.com/intermediate/activities/president.htm (26 June 2003).
  These are good activities to create a mock presidential election in the classroom.

- Texas Bluebonnet Award Committee. "So You Want to Be President?" *Texas Library Association*, http://www.txla.org/groups/tba/activities/president.html (22 June 2003).

This is a well-done site because it is concise and to the point. The suggested activities are excellent to use to extend the story, such as researching presidents, making timelines of presidents' lives, and learning more about elections. Click on "Authors" to learn more about Judith St. George and see links to related sites to expand the story.

- Works, Pam Bruns. "TeacherView: So You Want to Be President?" *Education Place, Houghton Mifflin Company*, http://www.eduplace.com/tview/pages/s/So_You_Want_to_Be_President_ Judith_St__George.html (21 June 2003).

This integrated lesson plan suggests ways to learn more about the job of the president through games, an online treasure hunt, and learning about the White House.

2000 *Joseph Had a Little Overcoat*
by Simms Taback

- Cornerstones. "Joseph Had a Little Overcoat," *Between the Lions, PBSkids.org, National Center for Accessible Media*, http://pbskids.org/lions/cornerstones/joseph/ (22 June 2003).

This amazing teaching unit has a downloadable lesson guide, printable activities, and links to five online games, and information about six different versions of the story with video clips. Be sure to click on the Hypertext Slide Show for this story. Print the Student Activity Workbook for numerous activities to use with the story. Adobe Acrobat and QuickTime are required to view the activities.

- Rourke, Jennifer. "TeacherView: Joseph Had a Little Overcoat," *Education Place, Houghton Mifflin Company*, http://www.eduplace.com/tview/pages/j/Joseph_Had_a_Little_Overcoat_ Simms_Taback.html (21 June 2003).

This lesson has a sequencing activity to use with the story and an excellent writing/art activity to produce a class book about being thankful using "cut-outs," much like the ones in the book.

- Smith, Nancy. "Caldecott Connections: Joseph Had a Little Overcoat," *Literature Learning Ladders, EduScapes.com*, http://eduscapes.com/caldecott/00a.htm (22 June 2003).

This site has good links to learn more about the author/illustrator.

- Smith, Toni. "Joseph Had a Little Overcoat," *Valdosta State University*, http://www.valdosta.edu/~tjsmith/paint.html (22 June 2003).

This colorful site suggests listing items which can be made from the overcoat.

- Smith, Toni. "Joseph Had a Little Overcoat Paint Lesson Plan," *Valdosta State University*, http://www.valdosta.edu/~tjsmith/paintlesson.html (22 June 2003).
This creative lesson plan effectively integrates technology through the use of a paint software program, such as *Microsoft Paint*, to create captioned illustrations.

- West, Angie, Jodi Stevens, Cheryl Delia, Valerie Bradshaw, and Mike Kahn. "Joseph Had a Little Overcoat," *Salisbury University*, http://faculty.ssu.edu/~elbond/overcoat.htm (22 June 2003).
This picture book project has many features to enhance the story: a book talk, an author/illustrator study, links to other sites about Simms Taback, integrated curriculum activities, and a web activity about recycling.

1999 *Snowflake Bentley*
illustrated by Mary Azarian, text by Jacqueline Briggs Martin

---

- Hurst, Carol Otis. "Snowflake Bentley," *Carol Hurst's Children's Literature Site*, http://www.carolhurst.com/titles/snowflakebentley.html (22 June 2003).
This is a good site to use in correlation with the book. There are many links to related activities to extend the story, such as sites about snowflakes and art connections.

- Lamb, Annette and Nancy Smith. "Caldecott Connections: Snowflake Bentley," *Literature Learning Ladders*, *EduScapes.com*, http://eduscapes.com/caldecott/99a.html (22 June 2003).
This outstanding lesson site has many features to expand the story. There are links to information about the author and illustrator, information on Wilson Bentley, links to sites about snowflakes, and much more.

- "Let's Talk: Snowflake Bentley," *FirstTeacherTLC.com*, http://familytlc.net/issues/january2003/books_8_441.html (26 June 2003).
This concise site has a good review of the book and an activity to discuss the two separate stories in the book.

- Libbrecht, Kenneth G. "Snow Crystals," *Cal Tech*, http://www.its.caltech.edu/~atomic/snowcrystals/ (26 June 2003).
View photographs of actual snowflakes from this amazing site. Visit the Snow Crystals Galleries and Photo Collections. Afterwards, have students design their own snowflakes. Hang from the classroom ceiling to display.

- Polette, Nancy. "Literature Guide: Snowflake Bentley," *Houghton Mifflin Company*, http://www.nancypolette.com/LitGuidesText/snowflake.htm (22 June 2003).
This literature guide has activities about the science of snowflakes, a discussion of other famous scientists, and a brief biographical sketch of Wilson Bentley.

- Smith, Katy and Heidi Weber. "TeacherViews: Snowflake Bentley," *Education Place, Houghton Mifflin Company,* http://www.eduplace.com/tview/pages/s/Snowflake_Bentley_Jacqueline_ Briggs_Martin.html (21 June 2003).

These two lesson plans suggest looking at pictures of snow crystals by going to the website about Wilson A. Bentley, using geometry to make snowflakes, and looking at crystals under a microscope.

- "Snowflake Bentley," *Mount Erie Elementary School, Anacortes, WA,* http://mte.anacortes.k12.wa.us/library/Caldecott/snowflake.htm (23 June 2003).

This page has reviews and commentaries about the story and illustrations.

- "Snowflake Bentley Quiz," *Cyberspaces.net,* http://www.cyberspaces.net/Nixon/AR/Snowfl.html (26 June 2003).

This is a set of questions to check students' comprehension after reading the book.

- "Wilson A. Bentley: The Snowflake Man," *Jericho Historical Society,* http://snowflakebentley.com/ (22 June 2003).

This is a must-see site to use with a study of the book. It contains enlargeable images of snowflakes as seen under Mr. Bentley's microscope and a video clip of "The Snowflake Man," a documentary about Wilson Bentley. There are many links to sites about snowflakes and related activities.

1998 *Rapunzel*
by Paul O. Zelinsky

- Hallen, Deborah. "Rapunzel," *Penguin Putnam, TeacherVision.com, Family Education Network,* http://www.teachervision.com/lesson-plans/lesson-5238.html (22 June 2003).

This plan gives page-by-page discussion questions to use with the book and suggests writing an advertisement for the book, making a diorama, and planting rampion seeds in a class garden.

- Lamb, Annette. "Caldecott Connections: Rapunzel," *Literature Learning Ladders, EduScapes.com,* htttp://eduscapes.com/caldecott/98a.htm (22 June 2003).

This page has two ideas for using this book in the classroom: creating fairy tales using *Storybook Weaver* (or other software program) and looking at other Grimm fairy tales on the web. Use this site as a springboard for other activities, such as comparing this version of *Rapunzel* to other versions.

- "Rapunzel," *Mount Erie Elementary School, Anacortes, WA,*
    http://mte.anacortes.k12.wa.us/library/Caldecott/Rapun.txt (23 June 2003).
    This site provides detailed reviews and commentaries from different sources about the story and the illustrations.

- "Rapunzel Quiz," *Cyberspaces.net,*
    http://www.cyberspaces.net/Nixon/AR/Rapunzel.html (26 June 2003).
    Use this quiz after reading the story to check comprehension.

1997 *The Golem*
by David Wisniewski

- "AuthorChats Archive: David Wisniewski," *AuthorChats, Yozons, Inc.,*
    http://www.authorchats.com/archives/viewArchive.jsp?id=20010123David
    Wisniewski.jsp&t=David+Wisniewski (25 June 2003).
    This is the archived transcript of a live online author chat with the noted author.

- "Author Spotlight: David Wisniewski," *Education Place, Houghton Mifflin Company,* http://www.eduplace.com/author/wisniewski/activities.html
    (24 June 2003).
    This is a biography, an interview, and a commentary about the author/illustrator's techniques and style. There is a cut paper activity for students to learn more about his artistic methods.

- Vandergrift, Kay E. "A Study of the Golem, Illustrated by David Wisniewski,"
    Rutgers, The State University of New Jersey,
    http://scils.rutgers.edu/%7Ekvander/golem/index.html (21 June 2003).
    A review of the work plus discussion questions to use with the story are included on the site. A bibliography of other versions of this traditional tale is given. There are several links to other sites with information about *The Golem.*

1996 *Officer Buckle and Gloria*
by Peggy Rathmann

- "Activity Sheet: Officer Buckle and Gloria," *First Book, Wisconsin Public Television,*
    http://www.wpt.org/kids/firstbook/pdfs/buckle.pdf (26 June 2003).
    This site suggests inviting a police officer to the class and making safety tips for the classroom or the home. (Adobe Acrobat required.)

- Houghton Mifflin Reading. "Officer Buckle and Gloria," *Debfourblocks.com,*
    http://www.debfourblocks.com/lessons/Officer_Buckle_and_Gloria.html
    (26 June 2003).

This guide suggests pre-reading, during reading, and post-reading activities to extend the safety theme in the story.

- Hoyler, Laura and Meg Nicks. "TeacherView: Officer Buckle and Gloria," *Education Place, Houghton Mifflin Company,* http://www.eduplace.com/tview/pages/o/Officer_Buckle_and_Gloria_Peggy_Rathmann.html (21 June 2003).

Both of these TeacherViews suggest using this book when teaching a unit on safety. Good activities are included in the lessons.

- "Integrated Unit: Officer Buckle and Gloria," *Curriculum and Instructional Materials Center, J. Murrey Atkins Library, University of North Carolina Charlotte,* http://libweb.uncc.edu/cimc/integration/Units/BuckleGloria.htm (22 June 2003).

This lesson plan has activities for language arts, social studies, science, math, art, and library media. The lesson themes are safety, community helpers, and learning more about police dogs.

- Lamb, Annette. "Caldecott Connections: Officer Buckle and Gloria," *Literature Learning Ladders, EduScapes.com,* http://eduscapes.com/caldecott/96a.html (22 June 2003).

This site has many good ideas to use with the book, such as extending the story with a study of safety, learning about the author, and learning more about police dogs. There are many links to use for related sites.

- Limestall, Brenda. "Safety WebQuest Based on Officer Buckle and Gloria," *W. J. Zahnow Elementary School, Waterloo, IL,* http://www.monroe.k12.il.us/websites/blimestall/webquestcommunityhelpersand services.htm (23 June 2003).

This webquest enhances the story while emphasizing safety for children.

- Martin, Bryon, Trisha Simms, Laurel Lyda, and Zoran Popazivanov. "Community Safety Across the Curriculum," *ETMA Cohort, San Juan Unified School District,* http://cohort.csus.edu/sanjuan1/communitysafety/lessonplans.html (19 September 2003).

This thematic unit for grades K-2 offer lesson plans in math, language arts, science, and social studies to use with the book.

- Mertz, Lauren. "Safety Tips for Every Day," *Success Link,* http://www.successlink.org/great2/g1693.html (26 June 2003).

This lesson suggests Halloween safety ideas to implement after reading the book.

- "Officer Buckle and Gloria," *Reading Magically,* http://www.libsci.sc.edu/miller/Officer_Buckle.htm (23 June 2003).

This well-done lesson plan has many links about safety to use as extensions to the book. It also has activities to correlate with School Safety Month, America's Safe

Schools Week, and National School Bus Safety Week. There are links to other lesson plans about safety.

- "Officer Buckle and Gloria," *Mount Erie Elementary School, Anacortes, WA*, http://mte.anacortes.k12.wa.us/library/Caldecott/Officer.txt (23 June 2003). This page has reviews and commentaries about the book from different sources.

- "Officer Buckle and Gloria," *Scholastic, Inc.*, http://www2.scholastic.com/teachers/authorsandbooks/teachingwithbooks/ producthome.jhtml?productID=11804&displayName=Description (22 June 2003). Click on the discussion guide and extension activity links to access suggestions for this book.

- Smolkin, Laura. "Officer Buckle and Gloria," *Webbing Into Literacy: a Book-A-Week Classroom Instruction*, http://curry.edschool.virginia.edu/go/wil/Buckle_Lesson.pdf (26 June 2003). This is an excellent lesson plan to extend the story. It has activities about safety, cartoon art, and four printable accident pictures to use with the instruction. (Adobe Acrobat required.)

- "Story Extensions: Officer Buckle and Gloria," *Scholastic, Inc.*, http://click.scholastic.com/collateral/extension_activities/officerbuckle_ea.html (22 June 2003). This extension activity has a problem solving activity and a safety activity.

1995 *Smoky Night*
illustrated by David Diaz, text by Eve Bunting

- Lamb, Annette. "Caldecott Connections: Smoky Night," *Literature Learning Ladders, EduScapes.com*, http://eduscapes.com/caldecott/95a.htm (22 June 2003). Although a bit scant, this Caldecott Connection can be used as a starting point to extend the story. A good theme to use with this story is cultural diversity and acceptance and these topics can be added to enhance this lesson idea.

- "Smoky Night," *Georgia Center for Character Education, Georgia Department of Education*, http://www.glc.k12.ga.us/passwd/trc/ttools/attach/chared/lessonplans/smoky_nigh t.pdf (22 June 2003). This activity helps to teach tolerance, cooperation, and citizenship through learning about ancestors and from what country students' families originally lived.

- "Smoky Night," *Mount Erie Elementary School, Anacortes, WA*, http://mte.anacortes.k12.wa.us/library/Caldecott/smoky.txt (23 June 2003). This page is a compilation of reviews from many sources.

1994 *Grandfather's Journey*
illustrated by Allen Say, text edited by Walter Lorraine

- "Author Spotlight: Allen Say," *Education Place, Houghton Mifflin Company*, http://www.eduplace.com/author/say/# (24 June 2003).
This site has a biography, an interview, and gives an analysis of the themes and artwork used in his books.

- Bradley, Sandra. "Teacher CyberGuide: Grandfather's Journey," *San Diego County Office of Education*, http://www.sdcoe.k12.ca.us/score/grand/grandtg.html (21 June 2003).
This lesson integrates map skills such as finding distance on a map, learning about Japan, and creating watercolor paintings.

- "Grandfather's Journey," *Alta Murrieta Elementary School, Murrieta, CA*, http://www.murrieta.k12.ca.us/alta/grade3/grandfather/ (25 June 2003).
This site has a crossword puzzle, a word search, several online games, and links to other sites about Japan and Allen Say.

- "Grandfather's Journey," *Mount Erie Elementary School, Anacortes, WA*, http://mte.anacortes.k12.wa.us/library/Caldecott/Grandfat.txt (23 June 2003).
This site has compiled reviews and commentaries about the book from notable reviewing journals.

- "Grandfather's Journey," *Scholastic, Inc.*, http://teacher.scholastic.com/lessonrepro/lessonplans/profbooks/grandfatherjn. html (25 June 2003).
This site has a writing activity and an origami art activity to extend the story.

- "Great Adventures: Grandfather's Journey," *Macmillan/McGraw-Hill*, http://www.mmhschool.com/student/reading/mhreading/3-1/3-1-1-2.html (22 June 2003).
One activity at this site can be especially helpful to use as an extension activity about immigration and Ellis Island. There is a link to the Ellis Island site.

- Lamb, Annette and Nancy Smith. "Caldecott Connection: Grandfather's Journey," *Literature Learning Ladders, EduScapes.com*, http://eduscapes.com/caldecott/94a.html (22 June 2003).
This Caldecott Connection begins with links to learn more about the author and illustrator. There are many links to web sites about Japan which can be used in a study about the setting in the story.

- "Making Multicultural Connections through Trade Books: Grandfather's Journey," *Montgomery County Public Schools,* http://www.mcps.k12.md.us/curriculum/socialstd/MBD/Grandfathers_ Journey1.html (24 June 2003).

This lesson plan extends the story by having students make a timeline of events and study the habitats and modes of transportation found in the book.

- Smith, Katy. "TeacherView: Grandfather's Journey," *Education Place, Houghton Mifflin Company,* http://www.eduplace.com/tview/pages/g/Grandfather_s_Journey_Allen_Say. html (21 June 2003).

This lesson idea suggests that students conduct oral histories with family members and it has links to web sites about Japan and the author, Allen Say. Although it is intended for intermediate grades, it can be adapted for primary grades.

1993 *Mirette on the High Wire*
by Emily Arnold McCully

- "Mirette on the High Wire," *Alta Murrieta Elementary School, Murrieta, CA,* http://www.murrieta.k12.ca.us/alta/grade4/story1c/ (26 June 2003).

This site has links to word games, puzzles, a quiz, a review, and links to related sites to use in a literature study of the book. Although intended for grade four, it has many elements which can be used in lower grades.

- "Mirette on the High Wire," *Mount Erie Elementary School, Anacortes, WA,* http://mte.anacortes.k12.wa.us/library/Caldecott/Mirette.txt (23 June 2003).

This page has a compilation of reviews and commentaries about the book.

- " Mirette on the High Wire," *Scholastic, Inc.,* http://www2.scholastic.com/teachers/authorsandbooks/teachingwithbooks/ producthome.jhtml?productID=11318&collateralID=5387&displayName= Discussion%2BGuide (22 June 2003).

This web site has a discussion guide, an extension activity, a book talk, and links to an interview with the author and a biography.

- Smith, Katy. "TeacherView: Mirette on the High Wire," *Education Place, Houghton Mifflin Company,* http://www.eduplace.com/tview/pages/m/Mirette_on_the_High_Wire_Emily_ Arnold_McCully.html (21 June 2003).

This integrated lesson plan has a science activity to learn about balance, a picture book activity to compare different styles of illustration, and links to other sites about the author/illustrator.

1992 *Tuesday*
by David Wiesner

- Lamb, Annette, Larry Johnson, and Nancy Smith. "Caldecott Connections: Tuesday," *Literature Learning Ladders*, *EduScapes.com*, http://eduscapes.com/caldecott/92a.html (27 June 2003).
This site has many links to do an author study of David Wiesner and has links to informational sites about frogs and lesson plans about frogs.

- "Tuesday," *Mount Erie Elementary School, Anacortes, WA*, http://mte.anacortes.k12.wa.us/library/Caldecott/Tuesday.txt (23 June 2003).
This page provides reviews and commentaries about the book from reviewing journals.

1991 *Black and White*
by David Macaulay

- "Black and White," *Mount Erie Elementary School, Anacortes, WA*, http://mte.anacortes.k12.wa.us/library/caldecott/blackan.txt (23 June 2003).
This site has reviews and commentaries about the book from respected journals.

- Hurst, Carol and Rebecca Otis. "Black and White," *Carol Hurst's Children's Literature Site*, http://www.carolhurst.com/titles/blackandwhite.html (21 June 2003).
This well-known site has good suggestions to help students analyze and critique the book, especially the illustrations. The lesson also has directions for an art activity to create negative and positive images.

1990 *Lon Po Po: A Red Riding Hood Story from China*
by Ed Young

- Agha, Charlotte. "TeacherView: Lon Po Po," *Education Place, Houghton Mifflin Company*, http://www.eduplace.com/tview/pages/l/Lon_Po_Po_Ed_Young.html (21 June 2003).
This lesson provides discussion questions to use with the story, suggests comparing the story to the traditional *Little Red Riding Hood* story, and suggests a study of other Chinese folk tales.

- Andreoletti, Nancy, Brenda Seely, and Dotti Danforth. "Little Red Riding Hood and Lon Po Po," *UVM Asian Studies Outreach Program, Burlington, VT,* http://www.uvm.edu/~outreach/units/LonPoPo.pdf (26 June 2003).
  This literature study compares the traditional version, the Chinese version, and the Korean version. There are printable worksheet activities included.

- Cook, Bill and Mike Hranac. "Comparing Cultures," *Liberty Elementary School, ID,* http://education.boisestate.edu/interchange/lessons1999/comparingcultures.htm (22 June 2003).
  This is a good lesson plan to compare two versions of Red Riding Hood: the settings, characters, clothing, and endings. Then students are asked to write Chinese versions of other popular folktales.

- "Integrated Unit: Lon Po Po," *Curriculum and Instructional Materials Center, J. Murrey Atkins Library, University of North Carolina Charlotte,* http://libweb.uncc.edu/cimc/integration/Units/LonPoPo.htm (22 June 2003).
  Although this lesson plan is for higher grade levels, it can easily be adapted for primary grades. Suggestions include comparing the story with other versions of Little Red Riding Hood, learning about China, and writing newspaper articles from the story.

- "Lon Po Po," *Alta Murrieta Elementary School, Murrieta, CA,* http://www.murrieta.k12.ca.us/alta/grade3/lonpopo/ (23 June 2003).
  This site has links to a crossword puzzle, hangman game, online quiz, vocabulary and words, matching, concentration, flashcards, a word search, and related web links about China and fairy tales. The web link "About the Story" is no longer active.

- "Lon Po Po," *Mount Erie Elementary School, Anacortes, WA,* http://mte.anacortes.k12.wa.us/library/Caldecott/lonpo.txt (23 June 2003).
  Read reviews and commentaries about the book from this site.

- "Lon Po Po," *TeacherVision.com, Family Education Network,* http://www.teachervision.com/lesson-plans/lesson-8005.html (23 June 2003).
  This lesson plan has enrichment activities and web resources to extend the book. There are links to a Venn diagram, Chinese symbols, a Chinese word search, Chinese culture, and art activities. There is also a link to the traditional Grimm Brothers version.

- "Lon Po Po: A Red Riding Hood Story from China," *Scholastic, Inc.,* http://www2.scholastic.com/teachers/authorsandbooks/teachingwithbooks/producthome.jhtml?productID=11673&collateralID=5764&displayName=Teaching%2BPlan (22 June 2003).
  This site has a teaching plan to use with the book and links to a biography and interview with the author/illustrator. The teaching plan suggests exploring panel art and provides pre-reading and post-reading questions.

- Murphy, Melinda. "Lon Po Po,"
  http://web.bsu.edu/00smtancock/CyberLessons/LonPoPo/default.htm
  (26 June 2003).
  This well-done online exploration has many extensions to use with the story. There are many links to explore details about China, an online quiz, word search, and a link to a traditional version of *Little Red Riding Hood.* Although intended for fourth grade, the activities can be used with lower grades.

- "Quia Quiz: Lon Po Po by Ed Young," *Quia.Corporation,*
  http://www.quia.com/servlets/quia.web.QuiaWebManager (26 June 2003).
  This is an online quiz to use after reading the book. Also at the *Quia* site, go to Melinda's *Lon Po Po Vocabulary* for a *Lon Po Po* word search:
  http://www.quia.com/jg/126913.html.

1989 *Song and Dance Man*
illustrated by Stephen Gammell, text by Karen Ackerman

- Liz. "Song and Dance Man," *Teachers.Net,*
  http://teachers.net/lessons/posts/1532.html (22 June 2003).
  This is a guided reading lesson to use with a unit on family.

- "Song and Dance Man," *Mount Erie Elementary School, Anacortes, WA,*
  http://mte.anacortes.k12.wa.us/library/Caldecott/songand.txt (23 June 2003).
  This site has reviews and commentaries from well-known reviewing journals.

- "Song and Dance Man," *Scholastic, Inc.,*
  http://www2.scholastic.com/teachers/authorsandbooks/teachingwithbooks/
  producthome.jhtml?productID=11233&displayName=Description (22 June 2003).
  This site has links to an extension activity and a discussion guide to use with the book.

- "Song and Dance Man," *TeacherVision.com, Family Education Network,*
  http://www.teachervision.com/lesson-plans/lesson-2539.html (22 June 2003).
  This lesson plan suggests that students interview their grandparents and learn about different forms of entertainment. This would be a good plan to use while teaching music.

1988 *Owl Moon*
illustrated by John Schoenherr, text by Jane Yolen

- Agha, Charlotte, Mary Ruth Higgs, and Katy Smith. "TeacherViews: Owl Moon," *Education Place, Houghton Mifflin Company*, http://www.eduplace.com/tview/pages/o/Owl_Moon_Jane_Yolen.html (21 June 2003).
Three lesson plans are included on this site. Creative writing activities, art activities (draw a picture with one half in winter and one half in summer), making a graphic organizer, studying owls and endangered owls, poetry, and letter writing. There are links to a Jane Yolen site and web sites about owls.

- Gordon, Amy. "The Who's Who of Owl Moon," *TechConnections.net*, http://www.techconnections.net/agordon/udel/lesson.pdf (26 June 2003).
This integrated lesson plan utilizes Kidspiration to create a graphic organizer and oral presentation for the story. Students also learn about story elements in this lesson. (Adobe Acrobat required.)

- The Kennedy Center ArtsEdge. "An Owl in the Woods," http://artsedge.kennedy-center.org/teaching_materials/curricula/curriculum.cfm?curriculum_id=268&mode=full (26 June 2003).
This literature plan has language arts and art activities to use with the book. There is a link to a scoring rubric and a link to another site to learn more about owls.

- Novak, Dawn and Bill Chapman. "Night Creatures," *Collaborative Lesson Archive*, http://faldo.atmos.uiuc.edu/CLA/LESSONS/1.html (26 June 2003).
This lesson plan extends the story through a study of nocturnal animals and the difference between diurnal and nocturnal animals. There is a link to a prerequisite lesson, "Day and Night," to use first to explain the science of day and night.

- "Owl Moon," *Mount Erie Elementary School, Anacortes, WA*, http://mte.anacortes.k12.wa.us/library/Caldecott/owlmoon.txt (23 June 2003).
This site has a compilation of reviews and commentaries from different sources.

- "Owl Moon," *Scholastic, Inc.*, http://www2.scholastic.com/teachers/authorsandbooks/teachingwithbooks/producthome.jhtml?productID=10418&displayName=Description (22 June 2003).
There are links on this site to a discussion guide, a teaching plan, extension activity, writing prompt, and an author biography and interview.

1987 *Hey, Al*
illustrated by Richard Egielski, text by Arthur Yorinks

- Tokar, Amy. "Lesson Plan: Hey, Al," *Penn State University*,
  http://www.personal.psu.edu/users/a/l/alt158/portfolio/lessonplan.html
  (22 June 2003).
  This lesson plan uses the book as the basis for creating paradise pictures.

1986 *The Polar Express*
by Chris Van Allsburg

- "Author Spotlight: Chris Van Allsburg," *Education Place, Houghton Mifflin Company*, http://www.eduplace.com/author/vanallsburg/ (24 June 2003).
  This site has a biography, an interview, details about the author/illustrator's works, and suggestions for classroom activities.

- Fischer, Denise. "The Polar Express," *Kinder-Themes*,
  http://www.kinderthemes.com/thepolarexpress.html (26 June 2003).
  This attractive site has activities for a Polar Express Day: Ride the Wish Train and Toy Train Counting Game.

- Freese, Lori L. "The Polar Express," *Collaborative Lesson Archive, University of Illinois*, http://faldo.atmos.uiuc.edu/CLA/LESSONS/2306.html
  (21 June 2003).
  This lesson plan uses a sleigh bell wrapped in a box to introduce the story and includes an art activity to use after reading the book aloud.

- "Integrated Unit: The Polar Express," *Curriculum and Instructional Materials Center, J. Murrey Atkins Library, University of North Carolina Charlotte*,
  http://libweb.uncc.edu/cimc/integration/Units/PolarExp.htm (22 June 2003).
  Two lesson plans are presented here. They both have good activities to extend the story, such as learning about trains, writing stories about a train ride, making a bell necklace, studying other books by the author, and finding the North Pole on a map.

- "Math Stories: The Polar Express," *MathStories.com, San Jose, CA*,
  http://www.mathstories.com/Christmas/Xmas_sheet_3_Polar_Express.htm
  (26 June 2003).
  Ten math word problems to solve are given to integrate math with literature. Note: The math problems are available to members only; refer to the copyright disclosure statement on the web site prior to using this site.

- "The Polar Express," *Mount Erie Elementary School, Anacosta, WA,*
  http://mte.anacortes.k12.wa.us/library/caldecott/polarexp.htm (23 June 2003).
  This site contains a review and commentary about the illustrations in the book.

- Smith, Katy and Heidi Weber. "TeacherView: The Polar Express,"
  Education Place, Houghton Mifflin Company,
  http://www.eduplace.com/tview/tviews/p/polarexpress.html (21 June 2003).
  Students will draw a picture of what they see out of the train window, they can visit
  links about Santa Claus, locate the North Pole on a map, and write a letter to Santa.

- "Favorite Gift Reproducible," *Trumpet Club,*
  http://trumpetclub.com/early/reproducibles/files/TREY_12.pdf (26 June 2003).
  This art activity to draw a favorite gift inside the gift-wrapped box would be a good
  activity to use with the story.

1985 *Saint George and the Dragon*
illustrated by Trina Schart Hyman, text retold by Margaret Hodges

- Buchanan, Matt. "Saint George and the Dragon," *Children's Theatre/Creative
  Drama,* http://www.childdrama.com/dragon.html (22 June 2003).
  This lesson plan has good discussion questions to use with the book and an art
  activity to make a dragon.

- Ortakales, Denise. "Trina Schart Hyman," *Women Children's Book Illustrators,*
  http://www.ortakales.com/illustrators/Hyman.html (24 June 2003).
  This is an excellent biography about the illustrator with much background information
  about her style and techniques in illustration. There are many links to other sites about
  the illustrator and her works.

1984 *The Glorious Flight: Across the Channel with Louis Blériot*
by Alice and Martin Provensen

- "The Glorious Flight: Across the Channel with Louis Blériot," *Scholastic, Inc.,*
  http://teacher.scholastic.com/lessonrepro/lessonplans/profbooks/glorious.htm
  (24 June 2003).
  This integrated lesson plan helps students analyze the illustrations and learn about the
  early twentieth century.

1982 *Jumanji*
by Chris Van Allsburg

- Alexander, Betty. "TeacherView: Jumanji," *Education Place, Houghton Mifflin Company*,
  http://www.eduplace.com/tview/pages/j/Jumanji_Chris_Van_Allsburg.html
  (21 June 2003).
  This lesson extends the story by incorporating a study of rainforests and other habitats.

- Hurst, Carol Otis. "Jumanji," *Carol Hurst's Children's Literature Site*,
  http://www.carolhurst.com/titles/jumanji.html (21 June 2003).
  This article gives a review, discussion questions, and activities to use with the book.

- Miller, Elizabeth B., "Integrating Jumanji into the Curriculum," *Making Connections on the Internet, University of South Carolina, Columbia*,
  http://www.libsci.sc.edu/miller/Jumanji.htm (25 June 2003).
  This integrated lesson plan has ideas for all subjects. It incorporates the study of volcanoes, the rain forest, links to information about the author/illustrator, and a jungle adventure board game.

1981 *Fables*
by Arnold Lobel

- "Fables," *Scholastic, Inc.*,
  http://www2.scholastic.com/teachers/authorsandbooks/teachingwithbooks/
  producthome.jhtml?productID=11663&collateralID=5385&displayName=
  Discussion%2BGuide (22 June 2003).
  This site has links to a discussion guide and extension activity to use with the book.

- Hoyler, Laura and Katy Smith. "TeacherViews: Fables," *The Education Place, Houghton Mifflin Company*,
  http://www.eduplace.com/tview/pages/f/Fables_Arnold_Lobel.html
  (21 June 2003).
  Two lessons are presented here, both with good ideas to use with the story, such as comparing the fables to those of Aesop.

1980 *Ox-Cart Man*
illustrated by Barbara Cooney, text by Donald Hall

- Grubb, Libby. "You Have to Give Up Something!" *LessonPlansPage.com*, http://www.lessonplanspage.com/SSOpportunityCosts23.htm (22 June 2003). This lesson plan teaches the term "opportunity cost" (items that are given up in order to receive something else) as it relates to the story.

- Harvey, Linda F. and Katy Smith. "TeacherView: Ox-Cart Man," *Education Place, Houghton Mifflin Company*, http://www.eduplace.com/tview/pages/o/OxCart_Man_Donald_Hall.html (26 June 2003). These lesson plans suggest extending the story with a study of pioneer life.

- KidsEconBooks. "Lesson: Ox-Cart Man," *ICEE and The School Book Center*, http://www.kidseconbooks.com/html/ox-cart_man.html (26 June 2003). This economics lesson discusses goods, services, and consumers to extend the story.

- LeBlanc, Meredith and Barbara Nanni. "Teacher CyberGuide: The Ox-Cart Man," *Metro Nashville Public Schools, TN*, http://www.nashville.k12.tn.us/CyberGuides/Brookmeade/nanni.html (21 June 2003). This lesson plan integrates the study of the seasons with the setting in the story. There are links to Portsmouth, New Hampshire, the setting in the story, graphic organizers, and activities pursued during the time period in the story, such as candle making, maple syrup making, and journal writing.

- Lewis, Gale C., "Lesson Plan for Ox-Cart Man," http://www.bchs.k12.va.us/Technology%20Class/lewis/Lesson_Plans/Lesson_Plan_for_Ox_Cart_Man.pdf (26 June 2003). This lesson plan incorporates the economics concepts of goods, capital resources, human resources, and natural resources. A Venn diagram is included.

- Ortakales, Denise. "Barbara Cooney," *Women Children's Book Illustrators*, http://www.ortakales.com/illustrators/Cooney.html (24 June 2003). This is a very good biography of the author and commentary about her style and techniques in illustration. There is a link that explains her scratchboard technique and a link to a *Horn Book* essay on her illustrations.

- "Ox-Cart Man," *Progeny Press*, http://www.progenypress.com/samples/pdf/oxcart.pdf (26 June 2003). This lesson plan has language arts printables to use as activity sheets to extend the story. The activities include keeping a weather journal, making a chart of monthly tasks, which occurred in the story, a synonym activity, and a dictionary activity. (Adobe Acrobat is required.)

- "Ox-Cart Man," *Scholastic, Inc.*,
  http://www2.scholastic.com/teachers/authorsandbooks/teachingwithbooks/product
  home.jhtml?productID=11308&displayName=Description (22 June 2003).
  This site has a teaching plan and discussion guide to use with the story.

- Reading Rainbow. "Ox-Cart Man," *GPN*, http://gpn.unl.edu/guides/rr/18.pdf
  (26 June 2003).
  This is the Teacher's Guide to the story from the popular Reading Rainbow series. It
  has many good activities to extend the story, such as comparing modern day chores
  with those of pioneer children, discussing the different tasks that occurred with the
  changing seasons, and learning about pioneer and colonial life. See also:
  http://gpn.unl.edu/guides/rr/018ss.pdf for a related set of social studies activities to
  use with the book. See also: http://gpn.unl.edu/guides/rr/18math.pdf for related math
  activities.

1979 *The Girl Who Loved Wild Horses*
   by Paul Goble

- "The Girl Who Loved Wild Horses," *Scholastic, Inc.*,
  http://www2.scholastic.com/teachers/authorsandbooks/teachingwithbooks/product
  home.jhtml?productID=10118&collateralID=5403&displayName=
  Discussion%2BGuide (22 June 2003).
  This site has links to a discussion guide and an extension activity to use with the
  book.

1977 *Ashanti to Zulu: African Traditions*
   illustrated by Leo and Diane Dillon, text by Margaret Musgrove

---

- Weber, Heidi. "TeacherView: Ashanti to Zulu," *Education Place, Houghton Mifflin
  Company*, http://www.eduplace.com/tview/pages/a/Ashanti_to_Zulu__African_
  Traditions_Margaret_Musgrove.html (21 June 2003).
  This lesson plan suggests using the book as a basis for a unit on Africa. Ideas are
  provided to include in the unit, such as studying the countries in Africa, reading
  African folktales, and learning about African textiles and fashion accessories.

1976 *Why Mosquitoes Buzz in People's Ears*
illustrated by Leo and Diane Dillon, text retold by Verna Aardema

- Agha, Charlotte. "TeacherView: Why Mosquitoes Buzz in People's Ears," *Education Place, Houghton Mifflin Company*, http://www.eduplace.com/tview/pages/w/Why_Mosquitoes_Buzz_in_Peoples_Ears_Verna_Aardema.html (21 June 2003).
  This lesson plan teaches about cause and effect and suggests that students make a story web of the characters and write and illustrate a new story with three new animals.

- Bradford, Rebecca. "Why Mosquitoes Buzz in People's Ears," *SuccessLink, Jefferson City, MO,* http://www.successlink.org/great2/g1155.html (26 June 2003).
  This five-day lesson plan has good language arts and art activities to extend the story. Printable worksheets are included.

- Kennedy, Gerl, Meg Nicks, and Katy Smith. "TeacherViews: Why Mosquitoes Buzz in People's Ears," *Education Place, Houghton Mifflin Company*, http://www.eduplace.com/tview/pages/w/Why_Mosquitoes_Buzz_in_People_s_Ears_Verna_Aardema.html (21 June 2003).
  These lesson ideas include studying onomatopoeia, illustrating a favorite scene from the story, and an art activity with cause and effect.

- Reinfert, Kristin. "Why Mosquitoes Buzz in People's Ears," *Richland County School District One, SC,* http://www.richlandclicks.org/Teacher/connections/grade3/cause_effect.htm (26 June 2003).
  This is an excellent cause and effect activity to use with the book.

- "Why Mosquitoes Buzz in People's Ears," *Scholastic, Inc.,* http://www2.scholastic.com/teachers/authorsandbooks/teachingwithbooks/producthome.jhtml?productID=11072&displayName=Description (22 June 2003).
  This site has links to a discussion guide, extension activities, biographical information about the illustrators, and an interview.

- "Why Mosquitoes Buzz in People's Ears Word Puzzle," *TeacherVision.com, Family Education Network,* http://www.teachervision.com/lesson-plans/lesson-8415.html (23 June 2003).
  This printable worksheet is free and can be used as a language arts activity.

1975 *Arrow to the Sun*
by Gerald McDermott

- Cohen, Teena and Lisa Hamilton. "Teacher CyberGuide: Arrow to the Sun," *Metro Nashville Public Schools*, *TN*, http://www.nashville.k12.tn.us/CyberGuides/arrow/arrow.html (21 June 2003).
This lesson plan integrates the study of Native Americans with literature. Students will research Native American tribes and their homes, then prepare a Venn diagram to compare and contrast the homes. They will create original postcards showing the homes. Students will write an original Native American folktale and they will create a dictionary of Native American terms.

- Smith, Katy. "TeacherView: Arrow to the Sun," *Education Place, Houghton Mifflin Company*, http://www.eduplace.com/tview/pages/a/Arrow_to_the_Sun_Gerald_McDermott.html (24 June 2003).
This well-done lesson plan extends the story through a study of the Pueblo Indians. There is an excellent link to a map of the United States for students to see where the Pueblo lived. There is also a link to *Southwest Culture* and the author's web site.

1970 *Sylvester and the Magic Pebble*
by William Steig

- Burr, Carol, Valerie McAnally, and Shannon Taylor. "Teacher CyberGuide: Sylvester and the Magic Pebble," *Metro Nashville Public Schools*, *TN*, http://www.nashville.k12.tn.us/CyberGuides/Sylvester/tch.html (21 June 2003).
This lesson plan extends the story by studying rocks and minerals. There are many activities to go along with the unit and links to worksheets and graphics of rocks are included. Students will learn about the rock cycle, different kinds of rocks, and they will compare and contrast rocks.

- Dye, Renee. "Rocks and Sylvester and the Magic Pebble," *LessonPlansPage.com*, http://www.lessonplanspage.com/ScienceLARocks-SylvesterMagicPebbleCritique12.htm (20 June 2003).
This lesson plan extends the story by including a discussion of rocks and rock classification. It does not address the illustrations in the story but can be added to broaden the scope of the lesson.

1969 *The Fool of the World and the Flying Ship*
illustrated by Uri Shulevitz, text retold by Arthur Ransome

- "The Fool of the World and the Flying Ship," *Georgia Center for Character Education, Georgia Department of Education,*
  http://www.georgiahumanities.org/projects/char/reference/lessons/language arts/the_fool_of_the_world_and_the_flying_ship.pdf (22 June 2003).
  This brief PDF file uses the story to teach the character education traits cooperation, diligence, and kindness.

1967 *Sam, Bangs & Moonshine*
by Evaline Ness

- "Sam, Bangs & Moonshine," *Georgia Center for Character Education, Georgia Department of Education,*
  http://www.glc.k12.ga.us/passwd/trc/ttools/attach/chared/lessonplans/sam_bangs_and_moonshine.pdf (22 June 2003).
  This lesson teaches the character traits of honesty, loyalty, and creativity through an art activity.

- Snyder, Janice. "Sam, Bangs and Moonshine," *Harker.org,*
  http://users.harker.org/ls/JaniceS/litpage/book_pages/sam.htm (26 June 2003).
  This site offers a writing activity about the lesson Sam learns in the story.

1966 *Always Room for One More*
illustrated by Nonny Hogrogian, text by Sorche Nic Leodhas

- "Always Room for One More," *George Center for Character Education, Georgia Department of Education,*
  http://www.glc.k12.ga.us/passwd/trc/ttools/attach/chared/lessonplans/language_arts_lesson_plans_always_room_for_one_more.pdf (22 June 2003).
  This is a good activity to extend the story and discuss concepts of generosity, compassion, and respect for others.

- "Always Room for One More Quiz," *Cyberspaces.net,*
  http://www.cyberspaces.net/Nixon/AR/Always.html (24 June 2003).
  Use this brief quiz to check students' comprehension of the book.

1964 *Where the Wild Things Are*
by Maurice Sendak

- Ford, Terry and Ravenskye. "Where the Wild Things Are," *Fun Trivia*, http://www.funtrivia.com/quizdetails.cfm?id=21812&origin=1851 (26 June 2003).
Students can complete this online trivia quiz after reading the book.

- Gilboy, Lesley. "Where the Wild Things Are Thematic Unit," *Elko School, NV*, http://www.elko.k12.nv.us./northside/wild.htm (21 June 2003).
This integrated lesson plan has many different activities to extend the story including creative writing, art, and dramatization.

- Hoyler, Laura. "TeacherView: Where the Wild Things Are," *Education Place, Houghton Mifflin Company*, http://www.eduplace.com/tview/tviews/w/wherethewildthingsare.html (26 June 2003).
This top lesson plan has an imaginative art activity: making cooperative monsters.

- Powers, Pam. "Where the Wild Things Are: Sorting," *LessonPlansPage.com*, http://www.lessonplanspage.com/LAMathSSMDWhereTheWildThingsAre ComparingSortingAndIslandStudyK.htm (20 June 2003).
This lesson for early childhood grades, PreK-1, incorporates the story to teach classification, sorting, and math sets and subsets.

- Scholtes, Tina. "Max is Missing: an Elementary WebQuest," *Mississippi Department of Education*, http://teacherexchange.mde.k12.ms.us/teachnett/scholtes.htm (23 June 2003).
This first grade webquest has students creating graphs and costumes for the monsters so that Max can find his way home after being captured by the monsters.

- Szabo, Deborah. "Elements of a Story: Where the Wild Things Are," *LessonPlansPage.com*, http://www.lessonplanspage.com/LAWildThingsStoryElementsK2.htm (20 June 2003).
Use this lesson to teach story elements. Although the lesson does not incorporate a discussion of the illustrations, it can easily be expanded to include instruction about the illustrations and the Caldecott Medal.

- Yamnitz, Shelley. "Story Map: Where the Wild Things Are," *LessonPlansPage.com*, http://www.lessonplanspage.com/ReadingStoryMap.htm (20 June 2003).
This lesson plan teaches children about elements of a story.

1963 *The Snowy Day*
by Ezra Jack Keats

- Agha, Charlotte, Latresa Bray, and Katy Smith. "TeacherViews: The Snowy Day," *The Education Place, Houghton Mifflin Company*, http://www.eduplace.com/tview/pages/s/The_Snowy_Day_Ezra_Jack_Keats.html (20 June 2003).
  Three activities to use with the book are given: an art activity to create a winter scene, a science activity to observe frozen water or snow, and a dramatization.

- Berck, Helen. "The Snowy Day," *SuccessLink, Jefferson City, MO*, http://www.successlink.org/great/g72.html (26 June 2003).
  This lesson plan suggests discussion questions to practice critical thinking skills and classifying.

- Dalke, Jennifer. "The Snowy Day," *LessonPlansPage.com*, http://www.lessonplanspage.com/LATheSnowyDayComprehensionInferences12.htm (20 June 2003).
  This lesson plan uses the Caldecott award-winning book by Ezra Jack Keats to teach creative writing and inference.

- Fischer, Denise. "The Snowy Day," *Kinder-Themes*, http://www.kinderthemes.com/TheSnowyDay.html (26 June 2003).
  This lesson has students make predictions about different sizes of snowballs and graphing the results.

- Ford, Terry and Ravenskye. "KidLit: The Snowy Day," *Fun Trivia*, http://www.funtrivia.com/quizdetails.cfm?id=20671&origin=1851 (26 June 2003).
  This is an online quiz to take after reading the book.

- "Integrated Unit: The Snowy Day," *Curriculum and Instructional Materials Center, J. Murrey Atkins Library, University of North Carolina Charlotte*, http://libweb.uncc.edu/cimc/integration/Units/SnowyDay.htm (22 June 2003).
  Some very good activities are suggested at this site to extend the story, such as making snow people cookies, learning more about snow, making snowflakes, creating snow scenes, and writing snowman stories.

- "Keats in the Preschool Classroom," *Montgomery County Public Schools*, http://www.mcps.k12.md.us/schools/springbrookhs/keats/index.html (26 June 2003).
  This site has links to a biography about Keats, information about the Keats Foundation, and a flannel board lesson plan to extend the teaching of Keats' books. The lesson plan includes *The Snowy Day* as well as three other books by Keats.

- Noethe, Kathy. "Ezra Jack Keats Slide Show," *Germantown Elementary School, Montgomery County, MD,* http://www.mcps.k12.md.us/departments/isa/ga_gallery/keats.html (22 June 2003).

This is an amazing slide show created by first graders featuring the famous books of Ezra Jack Keats: *Jennie's Hat, A Letter to Amy, Peter's Chair,* and *The Snowy Day.*

- Reading Rainbow. "The Snowy Day," *GPN,* http://gpn.unl.edu/guides/rr/80.pdf (26 June 2003).

This Teacher's Guide from the popular PBS series has many good activities about snow and winter to use with the book.

- Smolkin, Laura. "Snowy Day," *Webbing Into Literacy: A Book-A-Week Classroom Instruction,* http://curry.edschool.virginia.edu/go/wil/Snowy_Day_Lesson.pdf (26 June 2003).

This outstanding literature guide has many activities to help extend and enhance the story. There are four activity cards covering winter, the seasons, learning about the author, and sequencing. At the end of the guide, there are full color activity cards, a photograph of Ezra Jack Keats, a newspaper article about the inspiration for the story, and a facsimile of the original Keats manuscript for *The Snowy Day.*

- "The Snowy Day," *Scholastic, Inc.,* http://www2.scholastic.com/teachers/authorsandbooks/teachingwithbooks/producthome.jhtml?productID=10985&displayName=Description (22 June 2003).

This site has a discussion guide to accompany the story.

1960 *Nine Days to Christmas*
illustrated by Marie Hall Ets, text by Marie Hall Ets and Aurora Labastida

---

- Gaines, Addie. "Fiesta Navidad," *Seneca Elementary School, Seneca, MO,* http://www.geocities.com/Athens/Aegean/2221/mexico.html (24 June 2003).

This lesson plan uses the book to begin a study of Mexico and the holiday Las Posadas. It has art activities and many excellent links to sites about Mexico.

1961 *Baboushka and the Three Kings*
illustrated by Nicolas Sidjakov, text by Ruth Robbins

- Smith, Katy. "TeacherView: Baboushka and the Three Kings," *Education Place, Houghton Mifflin Company,*
  http://www.eduplace.com/tview/pages/b/Baboushka___the_Three_Kings_ Ruth_Robbins.html (21 June 2003).
  This lesson plan suggests learning how Christmas is celebrated around the world and has students illustrating pictures from the story using the same style.

1959 *Chanticleer and the Fox,* illustrated by Barbara Cooney,
text adapted from Chaucer's *Canterbury Tales* by Barbara Cooney

- Ortakales, Denise. "Barbara Cooney," *Women Children's Book Illustrators,*
  http://www.ortakales.com/illustrators/Cooney.html (24 June 2003).
  This is a very good biography of the author and commentary about her style and techniques in illustration. There is a link that explains her scratchboard technique and a link to a *Horn Book* essay on her illustrations.

1957 *A Tree Is Nice*
illustrated by Marc Simont, text by Janice Udry

- "Arbor Day Lesson Plans, Thematic Units, and Activities," *The Teacher's Guide,*
  http://www.theteachersguide.com/arbordaylessonplans.htm (27 June 2003).
  This site has numerous links to accompany any unit of study on trees. It also has arts and crafts activities, clip art, and printables about trees, such as a tree shape book pattern, tree coloring pages, and a Venn diagram.

- Frazier. "Tree Unit," *Myschoolonline, Family Education Network, Inc.,*
  http://www.myschoolonline.com/page/0,1871,38059-140527-42-9907,00.html (27 June 2003).
  This integrated unit on trees can be used to extend the story. It includes making an *A Tree Is Nice* mini-book.

- Keeling, Linda. "A Tree Is Nice," *Louisiana Challenge Activities for the K-12 Classroom,* http://www.challenge.state.la.us/k12act/data/tree.html (26 June 2003).
  This lesson plan extends the story through a study of trees, Arbor Day, and protecting forests.

- Young, Carol. "A Tree Is Nice," *Warnell School of Forest Resources*,
  http://www.forestry.uga.edu/warnell/service/education/materials/lessonplans/files/
  K1Youngwp.pdf (27 June 2003).
  This lesson plan uses the book to introduce a study of trees. Students will find products that come from trees, do an art activity, and learn why trees are important. (Adobe Acrobat is required to view lesson.)

1956 *Frog Went A-Courtin'*
illustrated by Feodor Rojankovsky, text retold by John Langstaff

- "Children's Songs: Frog Went A-Courtin'," *The Teacher's Guide*,
  http://www.theteachersguide.com/ChildrensSongs.htm (27 June 2003).
  The lyrics to this traditional children's song are provided at this site. The teacher can use this to teach the song or produce a puppet play to accompany the song.

- Kurtz, Mary. "Frog Went A-Courtin'," *John Glenn Elementary School, Northside Independent School District*,
  http://www.nisd.net/johnww/Library/00Integration%20Units/John%20Glenn%20
  Special%20Ed/Book%20Lesson%20Plans.htm#3 (27 June 2003).
  This lesson plan gives background information about this old folk song.

1955 *Cinderella, or the Little Glass Slipper*
illustrated and translated from Charles Perrault by Marcia Brown

- Anderson, Karen and Rhonda Byers. "Who Needs a Fairy Godmother, Anyway? A Cinderella WebQuest," *Plainfield Schools, IN*,
  http://www.plainfield.k12.in.us/hschool/webq/webq121/ (25 June 2003).
  This webquest asks students to compare two versions of the story. It has a link to an online version and links to math activities, a student rubric, and a teacher evaluation chart.

- "Cinderella Quiz," *Cyberspaces.net*,
  http://www.cyberspaces.net/Nixon/AR/Cinder1.html (24 June 2003).
  After reading the book, students can answer the questions from this quiz.

- Guerrero, Rosario and Nancy Rauner. "Cinderella Around the World," *San Diego Unified School District Triton Project*,
  http://projects.edtech.sandi.net/king/fairytales/index.htm (21 June 2003).
  This webquest will delight students as they go on a quest to read different versions of the story and then create a KidPix (or similar software) story of their own version of Cinderella. There is a link to countries around the world with versions of the Cinderella story to help students with the webquest. A rubric is included.

- Hagen, Kim. "TeacherView: Cinderella," *Education Place, Houghton Mifflin Company*,
  http://www.eduplace.com/tview/pages/c/Cinderella_Marcia_Brown.html
  (21 June 2003).
  This TeacherView suggests that teachers compare this story to other versions of the story from other countries, writing a newspaper article, and making a graph.

- Roche, Ruthi and Lynn Ryan. "Cinderella, Cinderella, Cinderella,"
  http://projects.edtech.sandi.net/brooklyn/cinderella.html (21 June 2003).
  This is a webquest that teaches children about different versions of the Cinderella story to become "Cinderella Experts." Students will create their own Cinderella stories to complete the webquest. A rubric is included for evaluation.

1954 *Madeline's Rescue*
by Ludwig Bemelmans

- "Madeline's Rescue," *Scholastic, Inc.*,
  http://www2.scholastic.com/teachers/authorsandbooks/teachingwithbooks
  producthome.jhtml?productID=11874&collateralID=5678&displayName=
  Extension+Activity (26 June 2003).
  This activity suggests using blocks to practice sets, addition, and subtraction. There is also a puppet activity.

1953 *The Biggest Bear*
by Lynd Ward

- Henderson, Meredith. "Activity Two: Can a Bear Be Responsible?" *Franklin, TN*,
  http://www.ccle.fourh.umn.edu/Rules.htm (24 June 2003).
  Scroll down the page to Activity Two to see thought-provoking questions that deal with responsibility and animal rights. There are also directions for a puppet show.

1951 *The Egg Tree*
by Katherine Milhous

- "Easter Egg Tree Paper Craft," *DLTK*,
  http://www.dltkkids.com/crafts/easter/meggtree.html (27 June 2003).
  This site has a perfect art activity to use after reading the book. There are printable egg and tree trunk templates.

1950 *Song of the Swallows*
by Leo Politi

- "Historic Mission," *Mission San Juan Capistrano*,
  http://www.missionsjc.com/historic.html (27 June 2003).
  Read about this historic mission which is the setting in the story.

1949 *The Big Snow*
by Berta and Elmer Hader

- "The Big Snow: Let's Talk," *FirstTeacherTLC.com*,
  http://familytlc.net/issues/january2003/books_3_1643.html (24 June 2003).
  This site gives thought-provoking questions for pre-reading, during the reading
  session, and after reading. Two snowflake activities are included.

1948 *White Snow, Bright Snow*
illustrated by Roger Duvoisin, text by Alvin Tresselt

- "White Snow, Bright Snow: Let's Talk," *FirstTeacherTLC.com*,
  http://familytlc.net/issues/january2003/books_3_1288.html (24 June 2003).
  This site gives good discussion questions to use with the story and two activities
  about winter.

1947 *The Little Island*
illustrated by Leonard Weisgard, text by Golden MacDonald

- "The Little Island," *Georgia Center for Character Education, Georgia Department of
  Education*, http://www.glc.k12.ga.us/passwd/trc/ttools/attach/chared/lessonplans/
  LittleIsland.pdf (22 June 2003).
  This activity teaches tolerance, respect for environment, and respect for others
  through art. Students will make watercolor under-the-sea pictures.

1943 *The Little House*
by Virginia Lee Burton

- Levine, Corinne and Beth Sullivan. "TeacherViews: The Little House," *Education Place, Houghton Mifflin Company*, http://www.eduplace.com/tview/pages/l/The_Little_House_Virginia_Lee_ Burton.html (20 June 2003).
  Two plans are on this site. They both offer good suggestions for extension activities to use with the book. The ideas revolve around the themes of change, city houses vs. country houses, and seasons.

- Ortakales, Denise. "Virginia Lee Burton," *Women Children's Book Illustrators*, http://www.ortakales.com/illustrators/Burton.html (24 June 2003).
  This is a very good biography about the illustrator and gives information about her style, techniques, and contributions to children's book illustration.

1942 *Make Way for Ducklings*
by Robert McCloskey

- Agha, Charlotte and Corinne Levine. "TeacherView: Make Way for Ducklings," *Education Place, Houghton Mifflin Company*, http://www.eduplace.com/tview/pages/m/Make_Way_for_Ducklings_Robert_ McCloskey.html (21 June 2003).
  These two lessons suggest a creative writing activity, provide discussion questions, link to *Animal Planet* to learn more about ducks, and make a map of the Public Garden.

- Family Education. "Make Way for Ducklings," *Family Education Network, Inc.*, http://familyeducation.com/topic/front/0,1156,22-15319,00.html (26 June 2003).
  This site has links to arts and crafts activities, a quiz, and a writing activity.

- Gentes and Doug Collicutt, "Mallard Duck," *Sargent Park, Nature North Zine*, http://www.wsd1.org/SargentPark/SP%20animals/mal_duck.html (23 June 2003).
  This is a fact sheet, with pictures, about mallard ducks.

- "Make Way for Ducklings," *Georgia Center for Character Education, Georgia Department of Education*, http://www.glc.k12.ga.us/passwd/trc/ttools/attach/chared/lessonplans/ language_arts_lesson_plans_make_way_for_ducklings.pdf (22 June 2003).
  This activity has students writing their own adaptations of the story to reflect the character traits of respect, loyalty, and cooperation.

- "Make Way for Ducklings," *Scholastic, Inc.*,
  http://click.scholastic.com/teacherstore/catalog/product/product.jhtml?skuid=
  sku50554&catid=&catType=&src=BTB000153P0010100000 (22 June 2003).
  This site has links to extension activities and a writing prompt.

- "Make Way for Ducklings," *TeacherVision.com, Family Education Network*,
  http://www.teachervision.com/lesson-plans/lesson-1733.html (23 June 2003).
  This well-done lesson plan has an egg carton duckling activity, an alphabetical order activity using the ducks' names, and an activity of drawing a map of the setting in the book. There is also a link to a *Make Way for Ducklings* online quiz.

- "Make Way for Ducklings," *College of Computer and Information Science, Northeastern University*,
  http://www.ccs.neu.edu/home/huangx/literature/ducklings.html (26 June 2003).
  This e-story has the complete text of the book to read online.

- Ravenskye. "KidLit: Make Way for Ducklings," *FunTrivia.com*,
  http://www.funtrivia.com/quizdetails.cfm?id=20730&origin=5546
  (26 June 2003).
  This is an online quiz to use after reading the book.

- Robeson, Patricia King. "Geography/Economics Lessons: Make Way for Ducklings," *Montgomery County Public Schools*,
  http://www.mcps.k12.md.us/curriculum/socialstd/grade1/Make_Way.html
  (21 June 2003).
  This lesson plan teaches geography and economic terms and teaches community. There are links to transparencies to print out and use with the lesson. Skills are taught for cardinal directions and mapmaking. A study of community service helpers is included. Discussion questions accompany the lesson.

- Schon, Nancy. "Make Way for Ducklings Public Art," *Nancy Schon Gallery*,
  http://www.schon.com/public/ducklings-boston.php (23 June 2003).
  View a wonderful photograph of the Boston Public Garden's bronze sculpture of Mrs. Mallard and her eight ducklings.

- Thomas, Natalie. "Make Way for Ducklings Tour," *George H. Conley Elementary School, Roslindale, MA*,
  http://www.geocities.com/EnchantedForest/Palace/3314/tour1.html
  (23 June 2003).
  Take a tour of the Boston Public Garden, the setting in the book. See the swan boats and the ducklings. View full color photographs of a kindergarten class visit.

1940 *Abraham Lincoln*
by Ingri and Edgar Parin d'Aulaire

- Lamb, Annette and Nancy Smith. "Literature Learning Ladders: Abraham Lincoln," *Literature Learning Ladders*, *EduScapes.com*, http://www.eduscapes.com/caldecott/40a.html (21 June 2003).

This lesson plan for this award-winning biography of Abraham Lincoln has students create a timeline of Abe Lincoln's life, build a log cabin, plot the places Lincoln lived on a map, and link to other sites about Lincoln.

Title Index

Subject Index

About the Author

Marilyn Dover Newman has been an elementary school media specialist for the Broward County Public Schools since 1988. She holds a master's degree in library science from Louisiana State University and a bachelor's degree in elementary education from Texas Christian University. Mrs. Newman has taught media education courses as an adjunct instructor at Nova Southeastern University. She has authored numerous grants in the area of preschool literacy. Mrs. Newman lives in Coral Springs, Florida, and has two children, Stephanie and Michael. Her hobbies include reading mysteries, needlepoint, quilting, and attending concerts and plays.